A Soldier's Tale

Living and Fighting with the Green Berets

Michael G. Skelly

Eloquent Books

Eloquent Books
An imprint of Strategic Book Group
P.O. Box 333
Durham CT 06422
www.StrategicBookGroup.com

ISBN: 978-1-60860-918-5

Printed in the United States of America

To:

Lorrie, Seth, Joseph, and Peter

Contents

Introduction

I couldn't believe the starry night display. I witnessed everything from a mass to shooting stars. I never viewed such twilight majesty, and it was confusing. My celestial gazing usually ended in disappointment because of street light obstruction. I realized there was no illumination. It was pitchy, and there were no streetlights around. I wasn't on my Victorian porch in upstate New York.

The confusion dissipated enough for me to know I was nowhere near home and that I wasn't relaxing. My ears rang, and my limbs were as dazed as my thoughts. My body went through a shockwave of transition, this time changing the numb to tingle and the tingle to movement. The stars, darkness, numbness, confusion, and movement weren't anything close to my porch. This wasn't Bath, New York. I was in the middle of combat in Lwara, Afghanistan.

That son of a bitch just fired an RPG at me, and the grenade hit the barrier right next to my head. The concussion from the blast snapped my head back and gave me a neck stinger. I grabbed my weapon and jumped back up to my fighting position behind the barrier. The insurgent was one hundred yards down the hill when he fired the RPG at me. As I got back into position, I wanted to find him, and to my amazement, he was right in front of me. He was preparing to jump over the barrier. I don't know who was more shocked, him or me. I'm sure he thought I was dead from the RPG round, and I couldn't believe he made it up the hill so fast. His rocket launcher was pointed at the ground as he was preparing to jump over the barrier. I had my M-16 pointed directly at him. Neither of us did anything-we just looked into each other's eyes. He had the most evil look I had ever seen. His stare pierced deep into my soul and brought a chill down my back. This was not the first time I had been in a situation like this. Two separate times during my career as a police officer, I had drawn down on an armed individual, but I was able to resolve both of those situations without shooting. This time I knew it would be different. This insurgent was going to kill me, and I wasn't ready to die for my country. Then all of my training took over. I aimed and squeezed the trigger. A three-round burst went off, and the insurgent dropped to the ground. The bolt on my M-16 locked to the rear because I was out of bullets. Just as he fell to the ground, I saw three more insurgents right behind him. They were armed with AK-47s and they were preparing to fire at me. Just then, Corporal Morris jumped in next to me with the SAW (Squad Assault Weapon) and cut the three insurgents down. “Holy shit, sir, I thought for sure you were dead. That RPG went off right next to ya. Are you all right?”

“I guess I am. My ears are ringing pretty badly. I need some ammo; I'm out.”

“Here, sir, take these.” Morris tossed me two magazines, and I reloaded my weapon. There were rounds zipping all over, everyone was shooting, it was total chaos. I began to scan for more insurgents. Then we heard the roar of the F-16s' jet engines. There was a bright flash then a thundering explosion as they dropped their five-hundred-pound bombs on the attacking insurgents. I got behind the barrier to protect myself from the blast of the bombs. As I sat there, I thought back to how my life had so drastically changed in just a year.

In August 2001, my wife and I had purchased the house of our dreams, a big, historic Queen Anne Victorian. We both loved the big old Victorian houses, but for many years we just couldn't afford one as we raised a family on a police officer's salary. Lorrie, my wife, stayed home with our three preschool sons, and I worked two to three jobs to make ends meet. When all three boys went to school, Lorrie went back to work. She got a job in county government, and I went on to a career as a school administrator. We were now financially set and able to afford the house of our dreams.

I was the assistant principal for a middle school in upstate New York. It was 9:00 a.m., September 11, 2001; I told my secretary that I needed to run to the bank. We had just closed on our old house the night before, and I wanted to deposit the check we got from the closing. On the way to the bank, I thought about how lucky we were to sell our old house so fast and what a great feeling it was to have finally made it to the place we wanted to be. I didn't have to work two jobs anymore to make ends meet. I had over twenty years in the Army Reserve, and I was eligible to retire. With our kids becoming more involved in sports and other school activities, I wanted to spend more time with them. My weekend reserve drills and administrative meetings each month were taking up a lot of time away from home, so Lorrie and I talked, and we decided it was time for me to retire. It had been a long time coming, but now I was really excited about stepping back and enjoying my family. When I got to the bank, I could see that the tellers were standing in a group talking; they all had a concerned look on their faces. When the teller walked over to wait on me, she asked me if I had heard the news that a plane had crashed into the World Trade Center. I was surprised; I told her no, I didn't know that. When I got back into my car, I turned the radio on and listened to the news broadcast on my way back to school. By the time I made it back to school, the news was out, and everyone knew the United States was under attack.

It was very chaotic at school. Our principal came running out of her office, crying. She said that her brother worked at the World Trade Center, and her family couldn't get in touch with him. I put my arm around her and walked her into the nurse's office. We tried comforting her. I explained to her that, with everything going on, I was sure that cell phone service and telephone service was disrupted, and that was probably why they couldn't get in touch with him. Teachers were huddled together in the teacher's lounge, watching the events unfold. The district office directed us not to let our students outside for recess.

Our school superintendent called for an emergency meeting after school of all school administrators. We met in the district office and discussed the events of the day. The superintendent knew that I was in the Army Reserve, and she asked me if I had heard anything. I told her I hadn't yet, but I was going to call the reserve center to find out what, if any, information they had. That night on my ride home from work, the excitement that I had earlier in the day, thinking about how we had finally made it, was now gone. I knew my military career was not ending but was about to take a new direction.

1

The Early Years

The success that I have had in life, my core beliefs, and principles came from the lessons taught to me by my parents. My father, Carolus "Red" Skelly, grew up in Elmira, New York, during the depression. He was an outstanding athlete, lettering in basketball, boxing, and football; in any sport he played, he excelled. He took up golf later in life when he was in his thirties and became one of the best golfers in the area. He was competing for club championships well into his late fifties, but it was football where he made a name for himself. He was a powerful fullback and a hard-hitting, aggressive linebacker. In 1935, his senior year, his football team won the Eastern High School football championship, and they traveled to Miami, Florida, to play Miami High in the high school Coconut Bowl, which they won 13–0. I would listen to his gridiron stories; he would always tell me that he wasn't the biggest or fastest on the team, but he made up for it with determination and hard work. He had a chance for a scholarship to Penn State, but he needed to get his grades up, so he went to Manlius Military Prep School where he again became a standout football player.

In 1941, the Army drafted him, but because of his football prowess, the Army assigned him to Fort Monmouth, New Jersey, home of the Signal Corps. For three years, he was a blocking back on one of the top service teams, which featured several former major college stars. There he was knocking heads with the best and more than holding his own. In 1944, he went overseas where he served in France and Germany as a member of the Signal Corps.

He was the most competitive person I ever knew. I remember when I was fourteen years old and on my high school golf team, I thought I was a pretty good player. I started bragging to my father about how good I was. I had just gotten paid for a lawn mowing job, and my father bet me that money that he could beat me just using a putter. I laughed at him and took the bet. I remember the determination and the focus he had that day. I had never seen that before in him, or anyone else, for that matter. By the end of the round, he beat me by two strokes and took my money. He told me to never bet unless it is a sure thing.

From that day on, I have always measured myself to him. Whatever I have been involved in, I always had to be the best, whether I was on the golf course, going to college, on patrol in a police car, serving in the Army, monitoring students in school, or being a dad and a husband. I learned the lesson many years ago that if you have the focus, determination, and belief in yourself, anything is possible. My father died thirty-five years ago, and he never got to see my success, but those lessons he taught me have been with me my whole life.

My mother, Donna Gordnier Skelly, also grew up during the depression. She was the second of four children; her parents divorced when she was a young child. Her mother couldn't afford to raise all four children, so her aunt and uncle raised my mother. She was the salutatorian for her graduating class of 1943. She moved to Elmira to attend the Elmira Business Institute. It was here, in Elmira, that she met my father after the war. My parents moved to Bath, New York, and my mother went to work for a prominent Bath lawyer as his legal secretary. My mother was a hard worker and dedicated to him. He became involved in politics and successfully ran for several judgeships. In 1972, he ran for the highest court in New York State, the Court of Appeals. My mother put in many long hours during his campaigns. I saw the importance of working hard and being dedicated to your job. I have followed those same principles all my life.

As a child in the 1960s, my favorite pastime was playing army. That was the heyday for shows like "Combat" and "The Rat Patrol," two of my favorite television shows. My father and all of my uncles served in World War II. I used to love to listen to my father tell me stories about his time in the war. He brought home several souvenirs from the war, and he would tell me how he took them from the Germans. One of my favorite souvenirs he brought home was a pair of

German antiaircraft binoculars. We had a small summer cottage on Keuka Lake, and I would sit by the hour on the picnic table, looking through the binoculars to the other side of the lake. I would imagine what it was like as the German soldier actually used them in combat. I also remembered my mother telling me stories about her brother, who was in the Marines and fought in the Pacific. She kept a scrapbook of newspaper clippings on the different battles he fought in. I couldn't wait until I grew up so I could become a soldier, too.

I graduated high school in 1976. I didn't know what I wanted to do, but several of my friends wanted to go to the local community college and take criminal justice. They all wanted to become police officers, and they convinced me to do the same. During my first semester at college, I spent more time in the commons than I did in class. My grades were terrible, and I figured I was wasting time with criminal justice. The next semester, I tried business administration but had the same result, and I realized I wasn't ready for college. By May 1979, I still had no idea what I wanted to do; I had bounced around from job to job. One day I found myself walking past the recruiting office. I stopped and went back to look at the poster. I began thinking about the stories my father used to tell me. I decided to walk in and see what they had to offer.

The recruiter was really friendly, and he could tell I was very unsure whether this was something I really wanted to do. We talked for a while about what the Army was like, and he told me, "This is the new Army. It's a lot better now than it used to be." Of course I had no idea what it used to be like, but he made it sound good. I told him I had taken some courses in business administration in college, and he said he had a job for me. He told me if I signed up then, he could get me a job as an administrative specialist. I asked him what that was, and he said it was a lot like what I was doing in college. I thought that sounded pretty good, must be I would be in charge of some kind of business aspect of the Army. My recruiter was very vague; he had a good reason to be, because an administrative specialist was just a fancy name for a clerk typist. I was about to become Radar O'Riley. He told me the enlistment would be for two years active and four years reserve duty. I thought about it for a minute. I remembered that, growing up, I always wanted to be a soldier, and I was sick and tired of bouncing around from job to job, so I told him I would join. Two days later, I shipped off to Fort Dix, New Jersey, and basic training.

Basic training was tough, but I loved the military. The Army was teaching me how to focus and become self-disciplined, something that I was lacking. I found the strength and determination that I saw in my father. At weapons qualification, I scored the highest in the platoon; I also qualified as an expert with the hand grenade, and I scored the maximum points in the physical fitness test. I was the honor graduate for our basic training company.

I left Fort Dix and went to Fort Jackson, South Carolina, for the administrative specialist course. It was here that I found out that an administrative specialist really meant clerk typist. We were going to learn how to write all different types of military correspondence. The major requirement for graduation was to be able to type sixty words per minute on the typewriter. When I was in high school, I took typing, and the best I could do was twenty-five words per minute. They told us the course would be self-paced, and it normally took the average soldier between four to six months to complete. I didn't like the idea of being a clerk typist, but I really liked the school. For every one male soldier going through the school, there were ten female soldiers. We had a weekend pass every weekend, and we spent it in Columbia, South Carolina. I had finished every requirement except for the typing part. After ten months in the school, the best I could do was forty-five words per minute. Finally, the sergeant in charge marked down on my test, "sixty words per minute." He congratulated me and sent me on. I finished up my active duty at Fort Belvoir, Virginia.

I came home in 1981 and began my reserve duty. I joined an Army Reserve Unit in Corning, New York, about fifteen miles from where I lived. The unit was a Combat Engineer Training Battalion. They didn't have a need for an administrative specialist, but they did need combat engineers. They sent me to Combat Engineer School at Fort Leonardwood, Missouri. When I got back from the school, I was assigned to a Drill Sergeant Company then sent to Drill Sergeant School. I really loved being a combat engineer. We spent a lot of time in the field, and for our two weeks in the summer, we would take over a basic training company at Fort Leonardwood. One of the other drill sergeants in my company was a police officer with the Corning Police Department. We got to talking one day, and I told him how much I hated my civilian job. He told me I should take the upcoming test for police officer. He said the police department was a lot like the Army. I really loved being in the Army, and I thought back to my days at Corning Community College. The only courses that I passed were the criminal justice courses. I decided that was a good idea, and I took the test.

I was hired by the Addison Police Department in 1982. Addison was a small village in the Southern Tier of New York, about five miles from the Pennsylvania border. It was a small police department, with only three members. Addison was known as a really rough town. At that time, the drinking age in New York was eighteen, and in Pennsylvania it was twenty-one. There were more bars than churches in Addison, and every weekend the bars filled up with Pennsylvanians coming to New York to drink. Being a small department, when I worked, I was by myself. If I needed help, my closest backup was twenty miles away. I learned many lessons in Addison, especially how to deal with violent individuals and how to keep a calm head in the most violent situations. These lessons would serve me well in the future.

I worked hard in Addison, and the word got out. In August 1984, the Chief of Police of the Bath Police Department came to Addison and recruited me for his department. It was a much bigger department, and it was in my hometown. There were always two officers on duty, and sometimes three. I was a patrolman for my first ten years. Just like in Addison, I learned many lessons there. I think the biggest lesson I learned was negotiation tactics. Twice, I became involved in a standoff with an armed and very agitated person. The first time, I intercepted a person who was on his way downtown to kill his boss. He had just been fired from his job. He went home, loaded his shot gun, and proceeded to walk back to his job, with the intent to shoot him. I caught up with him about a block from his job, in a small park. I took cover behind a tree and drew my gun. He stopped and turned toward me. He had his shotgun pointing to the ground. I knew I had no choice but to shoot him if he raised his shotgun. It was five in the afternoon, and the street behind me was busy with rush-hour traffic. I was able to talk to him and convince him to put his shotgun down.

The second time, I got a call to back up the state police, who had received a report of a gunshot in a motel just outside of town. We got to the motel, and the trooper knocked on the door where the reported shot came from. When the door opened, the man inside the room had a rifle and pointed it at the trooper's chest. The man's wife had left him, and he begged me to shoot him before he shot the trooper. This was January, and the temperature was twenty below zero. I was standing about ten feet behind the trooper in the parking lot. I drew my gun but, with it being as cold as it was and with my adrenaline flowing, I had a hard time keeping my gun steady. I had only a couple of inches between the trooper's head and the door to make the shot. I kept talking to the man in the room and eventually got him to let the trooper go. After about an hour of negotiations, he finally put his gun down, and we were able to enter the room and subdue him. These skills of negotiating with highly agitated people would again serve me well in the future.

Throughout my years with the Bath Police Department, I always did all the bicycle safety programs along with all the stranger safety programs at the school. The police department was seeing a rise in juvenile delinquency, and the school was experiencing a problem with truancy. The chief of police and the superintendent of schools decided to create a partnership to address these problems. They created the Juvenile Aide Officer position, and I was appointed to that in 1995. My job was to investigate all crimes committed by juveniles and assist school administrators in addressing their truancy problems, along with providing drug prevention and safety programs at the school.

As much as I liked working on the road patrol, I discovered that I liked working in the school better. I was getting tired of working rotating shifts and rotating days off; being assigned to the school gave me a permanent shift with weekends off. Lorrie was much happier with those hours, too. I had always thought about what I would do once I retired from law enforcement. After working in the school, I decided I wanted to go into education.

I went back to college part time and completed both bachelor's and master's degrees in social studies. In the summer of 1997, the school hired me as a summer school teacher. During the day, I taught 7th, 8th, and 9th grade social studies and at night I worked on the road patrol for the police department. The school superintendent knew that I was looking to make a change to education. She told me that, with my background in law enforcement and my experience teaching, I would be a great school administrator. She convinced me to pursue that path, but that required another degree in school administration. I continued on with my education and in 1999, I graduated with a Certificate of Advanced Study in education administration. My original plan was to teach social studies for a couple of years then apply for an administrative position. I applied for a teaching position at Bath; I also decided to apply for an assistant principal position with the Elmira City School District. I interviewed the same week for both positions and, to my surprise, Elmira offered me the job as assistant principal at one of their elementary schools.

I continued my service in the Army Reserves while working my civilian jobs. I really liked the Army and decided to make a career of it. In 1987, I received an appointment to the Empire State Military Academy Officer Candidate School. I graduated from the academy the following year and received a commission as an Infantry Second Lieutenant in the New York Army National Guard. I became the platoon leader for Bravo Company 2nd Battalion 392 Regiment 42nd Infantry Division. Being an infantry platoon leader was by far the best job that I had so far in the military. In 1989, I attended the Infantry Officer Basic Course at Fort Benning, Georgia. Again, it was another difficult school, but I worked hard and excelled. My previous experience as a combat engineer and drill sergeant proved to be very valuable in this course.

When I returned to my infantry company, I was highly motivated. I worked with my platoon on honing their infantry skills. Each year, the 42nd Infantry Division awarded the McArthur Award for the best combat-ready company in the division. General Douglas McArthur organized the division during World War I with the best regiments from twenty-six different states. McArthur said the division would stretch over the whole country like a rainbow. The division was nicknamed, "The Rainbow Division." We worked hard that year, preparing ourselves to win the award. I wanted my platoon to be the best in our company. During our two-week summer camp at Fort Drum, in August 1990, we went through a series of combat skill tests. Our company won the McArthur Award, and my platoon was the best platoon in the company. My platoon was designated the "Honor Platoon," and we represented the company at the award ceremony. Governor Mario Cuomo came to Fort Drum and presented the award to us, along with the commanding general of the 42nd Infantry Division. I accepted the award on behalf of the company. It was one of the proudest moments of my military career.

The day after we received the McArthur Award, we learned that Iraq invaded Kuwait. There was a lot of speculation on what was going to happen, and everyone started talking about being activated. We even had a television news crew come out to the field to interview us. Over the next couple of months, we were told to get our personal lives in order, because we were going to be mobilized. The Army was planning to pull forces out of Korea and send them to the Persian Gulf, and we would become the replacement forces for Korea. I couldn't wait to go; I was somewhat disappointed that we weren't going to go directly to the Persian Gulf, but if the war lasted long enough, I was sure we would get into the fight. That year, we trained harder than we had ever trained before. I wanted to make sure that my platoon was ready for war. As the months went on, I would read about more and more units that were being called up. I just knew that it would soon be our turn. Every time the phone rang, I thought that was the call, but the call never came. The ground war only lasted one hundred hours, with minimal casualties. We were never needed. I was terribly disappointed; all of our hard training and planning was for naught.

After the Persian Gulf War ended, I became disenchanted with the National Guard. The Army activated my old Army Reserve unit and sent them to Fort Leonardwood to train combat engineers. I wanted to be in a unit that had a real-world mission. As the Army Reserve and National Guard Units returned home from active duty, many of their members decided they had enough and got out. My old Army Reserve unit had an opening for a company commander. I called the battalion commander and told him I was interested in the position. He was new to the unit and was looking to rebuild it. Several of the officers left the battalion when they returned home. The battalion commander was in desperate need of officers and, with my previous experience as a drill sergeant in the unit, he hired me right away, and I became the Company Commander of Bravo Company.

The last time I was a member of the unit, I was an enlisted soldier. Now I was a commissioned officer. The respect enlisted soldiers show to officers who have prior enlistment time differs from that shown to officers with no such enlistment time. They know that an officer who was enlisted has been through the same basic training they experienced. They had spent their time as privates and pulled all the associated details. I had attained the rank of Staff Sergeant before I was commissioned, plus I had been through Drill Sergeant School. There were not many officers in the Army who wore the Drill Sergeant Badge.

One of my principles of leadership is to lead by example. Whenever we went to the rifle range, I always qualified as an expert; I always led physical training, and when there was a dirty job to do, I jumped in and helped out. I would never ask someone to do something that I wouldn't do. My soldiers knew this, and they were always willing to go the extra mile for me because they knew I would for them. Whenever we were in a chow hall or out in the field, I would always sit with my soldiers. I never portrayed myself as being better than they were just because I was a commissioned officer. These values I learned as an enlisted soldier, and the soldiers who served with me knew it.

I spent two years as company commander with Bravo Company. I received top evaluations from the battalion commander. He knew he could always count on me to handle any mission that was thrown at us. One year, the 98th Division picked a unit for a mock mobilization. They wanted to call a unit up on short notification, have them report to the Army Reserve Center, get their orders, then join an active engineer unit and participate in a field exercise with that active unit. The battalion commander called me and asked me to take the mission; he knew we would make the battalion proud. I gladly accepted the mission; I figured this would be the closest I would ever get to performing a real life mission.

It was about two weeks later when we got the call that we had twenty-four hours to report to the Army Reserve Center. We went through the process of having physicals, drawing field gear, and receiving the operation order. There were observers from Division Headquarters who reported on every step of the process. When we finished with that phase, we drove our trucks to Fort Drum and supported an active combat engineer unit from the 10th Mountain Division on a two-week field exercise. The active duty commander reported back to our battalion commander and division observers that we had exceeded his expectations for reservists. We were so good that we actually outperformed some of his active units.

During my tenure as Company Commander with Bravo Company, I became good friends with our Echo Company Commander, Rob Smith. In the civilian world, he was a fireman for the Elmira City Fire Department. He was a senior captain looking to make major. We didn't have any major positions open at our battalion, so Rob found a position with the 403rd Civil Affairs Battalion in Syracuse, New York. He left our unit in 1995, and I lost track of him. In February 1998, Rob called me; he was now the Acting Battalion Commander for the 403rd. He told me that several members of his unit just deployed to Bosnia in support of Operation Joint Forge, and he was looking for a detachment commander. A detachment commander in Civil Affairs holds the rank of major. I would be looking to make major in a few years, plus I had a chance to join a unit with a real-world mission. This unit mobilized and served in the Persian Gulf War, they sent a task force to Somalia, and now they have sent soldiers to Bosnia. I accepted his offer with no hesitation and became the Detachment Commander of Bravo Detachment 403rd Civil Affairs Battalion.

The mission of Civil Affairs is to act as a liaison between the civilian inhabitants of a war zone and the military presence. With their expertise in civil matters, they are the principal unit in assisting a commander in the conduct of civil-military operations. They keep the battlefield commander informed of the status of the civilian populace as well as effecting assistance to locals by coordinating military operations in the civilian populace; handling civilians on the battlefield; overseeing refugee operations; keeping the commander informed of protected targets such as schools, churches, hospitals, etc.; and interfacing with local and international Non Governmental Organizations and private volunteer organizations. This provides the commander with a unique battlefield overlay of all civilian activity, ongoing infrastructure projects, and the presence and mission of NGOs in the area. Ninety-six percent of the Civil Affairs personnel come from the United States Army Reserve and are usually tasked to support regular Army units upon mobilization. This allows combatant commanders to utilize reservists with civilian skill sets such as lawyers, city managers, economists, veterinarians, teachers, policemen, and other civilians who are more knowledgeable and better suited for restoration of stability and reconstruction tasks than soldiers from the active military. The remaining four percent of Civil Affairs personnel are active duty soldiers assigned to the 96th Civil Affairs Battalion, stationed at Fort Bragg, North Carolina. This is a rapidly deployable unit that supports the Army Special Operations Command. Active Civil Affairs are generalists, selected from around the Army.

I had eighteen years of experience as a police officer and two years as a school administrator. Those two experiences made me uniquely qualified for Civil Affairs. I stayed with the detachment until June 1999, when the soldiers mobilized for Bosnia returned. Rob asked me if I would take the Battalion Staff Officer S-2 position. The S-2 in the battalion is the Military Intelligence Officer. I really enjoyed being the S-2, but when Rob left the battalion in October of 2000, our S-1 (Personnel Officer) also left the battalion. Our new commander, LTC White, asked me if I would take over the S-1 shop. I was now about to come full circle with my military career. When I first joined the Army in 1979, I was an administrative specialist. I really disliked that job, and now I was going to take over as supervisor of all the clerk typists. I wasn't about to tell our new commander "no."

It turned out that being the S-1 wasn't as bad as I thought it would be. Actually, I really liked the job. I was fortunate that all who worked in the S-1 shop liked what they did, and they were very good at their jobs. The unit clerk and I shared many of the same responsibilities. Every three months, he and I would travel to Brigade Headquarters, located in Riverdale, Maryland, just outside Washington, DC, to give a briefing to the brigade commander on our unit status. I made a lot of contacts at brigade headquarters, which was the politically smart thing to do, since I was looking for a promotion to major.

2
Getting Ready

As soon as I got home from work on September 11th, I called the reserve center and talked with our operations officer. He said the reserve center was on lockdown. They had armed guards at the gate, and only those with military identification could get into the building. Those were the only orders they had right now. Our reserve drills were always the first weekend of the month, and we had just completed September's drill the weekend before. It would be a long four weeks until our October drill.

As I pulled into the driveway of the reserve center for our October drill, we had to drive around a series of barricades. As we entered the gate of the parking lot, we encountered four Marine guards. We shared our building with a Marine Reserve Unit. They were armed and performing one hundred percent identification checks. If you didn't have a military identification card, you didn't get through the gate. I had talked with our Battalion Executive Officer a couple of days before, and he said that, at 10:00 A.M., there was going to be an officer's call in the commander's office.

At our officer's call, Lieutenant Colonel White told us we needed to get things in order. The Army had instituted a "Stop Loss" order, and our unit was one of the units covered in that order. Stop Loss meant that soldiers in critical jobs could not retire or leave a unit. Civil Affairs was one of those critical jobs. Our training was now going to focus on mobilization. He told us that our Command, the

352nd Civil Affairs, had just activated a planning cell, and they were looking at contingencies. Being the battalion S-1, I briefed the commander of the 352nd every quarter on our unit readiness. We had a strong unit; the only unit in better shape was the 401st, out of Rochester, NY. I knew our commander would be pushing hard for our unit to get a mission. He told our supply officer to make sure we had all the equipment we were supposed to have; our military intelligence officer had to make sure everyone's security clearance was up to date; our training officer had to schedule us for weapons qualification, land navigation, and S.E.R.E. (Survive, Evade, Resist and Escape) training. My job was to scrub everyone's records, making sure everyone had a current evaluation, promotions were in, and immunizations were up to date. I also needed to schedule the battalion to Fort Drum for physicals. The colonel finished the meeting by telling us that it wasn't a matter of getting the call; it was just a matter of when.

Every drill physical training was scheduled for the afternoon. That Saturday, about six of us decided to go for a run. We all had on our physical training uniforms, which consisted of black shorts and a grey t-shirt with ARMY written on the front. As we ran down the road, cars would pass us and blow their horns. The people in the cars would wave at us and yell out the window, "Go get them," and "God bless you." This wasn't just one or two cars; it was every car that passed us. Nothing like that had ever happened before. I had always been proud of my military service, but that day I felt a real deep sense of pride that I had never felt before. We realized the great responsibility we had in restoring hope and pride to America.

Every day, I would go to the Department of Defense web site to see what units were being called up for Operation Enduring Freedom. That was the name given to the military operation in Afghanistan. It was three weeks before Christmas when I was checking the site, and there it was. The 401st Civil Affairs unit in Rochester had twenty people mobilized; if they were going, then we had to be next. The reality of what was happening really started to hit me. Every time the phone rang, I wondered if this was the call. It was the same feeling that I had during the Persian Gulf War.

Christmas 2001 was the first Christmas in our new house. Lorrie and I really enjoyed decorating the house at Christmas time. The kids were really excited about Christmas that year. We finally had a real chimney for Santa Claus to come down. The house was so big that we put up two Christmas trees. After we got all the lights up outside, we would walk across the street and look at the house. Everyone would tell us how nice the house looked. I tried to put on a happy face, but I couldn't enjoy it. I kept wondering what the future held. I didn't know where I would be next year or if this would be the last Christmas I would see. My wife and I didn't talk too much about it, but we had that same uncertain feeling.

As the months went on, our tempo at the reserve center increased. In January, we went to Fort Drum for physicals. Everyone who needed glasses got them, and those who needed the prescription inserts for our chemical masks got them. I had been in the Army now for twenty years, and this was the first time that I had ever had inserts for my protective mask. In February, we did a one hundred percent inventory of our equipment, and we ran a Middle East Orientation Course. It was designed to teach us the customs and courtesies of Muslim countries. In March, we concentrated on land navigation and did our SERE training. In April, we took the physical fitness test and the combat swim test. It was at the April drill that I found out that something was in the works. One of the detachment commanders came up to me and asked me if I would be on his team in the event of a mobilization. His name was Warren, and he was a senior major in the battalion. He was thirty-eight years old and a schoolteacher from upstate New York. Warren was a social studies teacher, and he had a garage where he worked on cars part time. He was married with two children. We became good friends; we had a lot in common, both of us being in education, and we both loved cars. We would always hang out together during drill. At the time, I was a captain, and Warren needed an assistant team leader. I asked him if he knew something about it. He said "no," but the battalion commander wanted him to put some preliminary teams together. The commander wanted us to start training together in our teams. Warren and I sat down that day and decided who we wanted on our team. I told him I wanted Steve, a thirty-five-year-old staff sergeant and police officer with the Syracuse Police Department.

Steve was a Navy veteran, having spent six years on active duty with the Navy. His passion was diving; he was a certified dive instructor and was always talking about the different places he had been diving. We gave him the nickname "Scuba Steve." We became good friends and spent a lot of time together at the unit. We were always swapping police stories. The Syracuse Police Department was a large department, and Steve had some real good stories. I called him a rookie, because he had only been on the force for five years, and I had eighteen years experience. He would laugh and tell me that he had done more in five years with the Syracuse Police Department than I had done in eighteen years with both Addison and Bath. The truth was that he was right, but I would never tell him that. Warren wanted Roger for Team Sergeant. He was a veteran of Operation Desert Storm. Roger was forty years old, single, and a construction worker. He had spent his entire military career in the 403rd. Warren liked him. He knew his job, and he had the experience of Desert Storm. We also picked Tim, a Specialist E-4 and recent graduate of Arabic school. Tim was twenty years old and single. He joined the 403rd right out of high school. He just returned to the unit from the eleven-month-long Arabic School. Tim wanted to go into law enforcement. He liked to hang around Steve and me and listen to our police stories. Our last member was Fred, a Specialist E-4. Fred was twenty-five years old and recently married. He had just recently joined the unit, but he had four years on active duty with the Infantry.

It was about 8:30 P.M. on May 20th, 2002, I was sitting at home watching television when the phone rang. I answered it, and it was Warren. He said, "Mike, we got a mission."

I wasn't sure I heard him right. "What did you say?" I asked.

"We're being called to active duty, we have a mission overseas." He didn't have many details, but we were going to be activated next month, and he would be the mission leader. He said that twenty-five of us were going to be activated. We talked for a few minutes. I kept asking him questions, but he didn't have any answers. He said, "We will be getting our orders in a couple of weeks," and that I should notify my employer. He told me that, as soon as he got more information, he would let me know. I had finally got the phone call that I had been waiting for. It had been eight months since the terrorist attacks, eight months of not knowing what was going to happen, but the waiting was now over, and I knew that I was going to war.

3

The Call Up

After I got done talking to Warren a, numb feeling came over me. I remembered back to 1990 and the Persian Gulf War. I so wanted to go to war then. I thought my unit would be activated, but as time went on, I realized it wasn't. I called National Guard Headquarters and tried to volunteer. They were looking for volunteers but not infantry officers. If I were a clerk typist, I could have gone, because there was a shortage of them—but not infantry officers. I was so disappointed that I didn't get to go, I was jealous of those who did. After I joined the 403rd, I would stay overnight at the reserve center, because I lived about 120 miles away. There were about ten other guys who would stay at the reserve center on drill weekends. We would all get together and go out for dinner, and then we would end up at the local VFW (Veterans of Foreign Wars). They were all combat veterans, some from Bosnia and some from Desert Storm. We would all sit around and tell war stories. The only problem was, I didn't have any war stories to tell; all I could do was listen. I had never even been overseas. My whole military career had been spent in the continental United States, but now that was about to change. The only problem was, I didn't really want to go; I was forty-four and married with three little kids. I had a great job and a new house. I thought, *why couldn't this have happened twelve years ago when I was single and wanting to go?*

I went back out to the living room where my wife, Lorrie, was watching television. I told her that the Reserves had phoned, and we were getting called up. It wasn't a shock; we had been expecting it for a long time. I told her, "It looks like we will be leaving sometime next month." I thought to myself, *I should have retired last year.* It was getting to be a drag driving to Syracuse every month, but I hadn't reached my goal yet of being promoted to major, plus I liked the extra money, and I really just liked being in the Army. The next night, Lorrie and I sat down and told the kids that Daddy was leaving with the Army and might be gone for quite awhile. Seth, our oldest, was ten, and he understood what was going on. Joseph was eight, and Peter was six. They knew I was in the Army but didn't understand the full scope of what was happening.

In June, we got our orders. We were leaving for Ft. Bragg, North Carolina, on July 12, 2002. We knew we were going to Afghanistan, but we weren't told what our mission was or what unit we would be supporting. It was very strange that we didn't know what the mission was or whom we would be supporting. On paper, our unit supported an Army Reserve Theater Support Group from Pennsylvania, but that unit hadn't been activated, so we were in the dark. Warren tried to get some answers so we could prepare, but nobody from our battalion or brigade knew what we would be doing. The only thing they could tell us was that we were going someplace in Afghanistan. The guys who had been through this for Desert Storm said this was completely different from what they went through when they were mobilized. They knew right away that they were going to support a Marine unit. No one could figure out why we weren't being told anything. It was making it really hard with our families, because we couldn't tell them anything. We were all getting very frustrated with the process.

At our June Reserve Drill, we had two soldiers from the 96th Civil Affairs Battalion come to our unit and give us a briefing on Afghanistan. This was the first time I had ever seen pictures of Afghanistan. I sat there as they were giving the presentation, and I just couldn't believe I was going to this place. They told us how there were extreme temperature swings from over one hundred degrees in the day to thirty degrees at night. Malaria, tuberculosis, and dysentery were rampant among the locals. They showed us some videos that they took while they were deployed. The biggest shock was that they had full beards and were wearing civilian clothes. They told us the reason they had beards was to show respect for the Muslim faith. What I saw and heard for the next three hours was completely foreign to me. All my military training was based around conventional military operations. I was an infantry officer and trained on infantry tactics. We would fight as a company with 120 soldiers, and each soldier had a specific job within the company. What I saw that day was unconventional warfare. These guys operated in small teams, far away from friendly lines. They were Green Berets specially trained to operate deep in enemy territory. I was glad to see what Afghanistan was like so I could start mentally preparing for it, and I was especially glad that we weren't a Special Forces unit. There was no way I wanted to operate in a small team deep inside Taliban country.

By the end of June, everything seemed to be happening so fast. In two weeks, I would be leaving for Fort Bragg. We were told that we would spend a month of training before we left for Afghanistan. Our tour of duty in Afghanistan was scheduled for nine months. We were due to return to the Untied States around June or July of 2003, but we could always be extended if needed—our orders were for up to two years.

Lorrie and I decided to go away for the Fourth of July. They had placed us on active duty the week before so we could pack everything at the reserve center and ship it to Fort Bragg. We had a long weekend off for the holiday, so Lorrie and I decided to take the kids to Gettysburg for the weekend. It was our last family trip before I left.

July 12th finally arrived. We had to be at the reserve center by 10:00 A.M. to load our gear. When we finished loading, we headed over to the airport. The family support group gave us a small going away party in one of the hangers with our families. When we got to the airport, our families were waiting for us in the hanger, it was almost noon, and our flight was scheduled for 1:00 P.M. The next hour was the worst hour I had ever spent. All I wanted to do was to hold Lorrie and the kids. I had never been away from them for more than two weeks. Now I was headed off to a war six thousand miles away, for up to a year. I still didn't know what our mission was or what part of Afghanistan I would be in, and I didn't know if I would ever see Lorrie and the kids again. The plane finally arrived twenty minutes late. Lorrie and the kids walked me to the plane, and we said our goodbyes. As we taxied down the runway, I could see Seth, Joseph, and Peter standing at attention and saluting the plane as we took off.

4

Fort Bragg

We arrived at Ft. Bragg around 3:00 P.M., and a bus was waiting to transport us to our training area. It was a short ride; our barracks were located in the old World War II section of Ft. Bragg, right next to Pope Air Force Base. Every time I had been on active duty for the Reserves or National Guard, I stayed in these old barracks. They were the same no matter what post I was assigned. They were built in the early 1940s, and they were exactly the same now as they were then. Each barracks consisted of two floors with open bays. There were rows of bunk beds in each bay, with lockers at the end of each bed. Each floor could accommodate forty soldiers. At one end of the barracks, there was a room for the commander, and at the other end were the latrines. They were ungodly hot in the summer and freezing cold in the winter. Our team decided to take the first floor, so I picked out my bunk and threw my gear in one of the lockers.

We boarded the buses again and transported to the training company's headquarters building. The training company was another Reserve unit whose mission was to certify us for combat. We gathered in one of the classrooms, where we were greeted by their commanding officer, Lieutenant Colonel Morales. He welcomed us to Fort Bragg and gave us a briefing of what to expect for the next three weeks. We were going to have first aid training, fire and maneuver training, land mine warfare, chemical and biological training, communications, and weapons qualification. We also had to do a health screening, physicals, and vaccinations. Upon completion of all these tasks, we would be certified as combat ready and given a departure date for Afghanistan. I thought to myself that this was going to be a real waste of time. The training they were going to give us was the same generic training all soldiers get in basic training. These trainers were just reservist, and none of them had ever deployed before. They can't tell us what it is like there or what the enemy is like or what we can expect. I remember reading stories abut the Korean War and how ill-equipped and unprepared the soldiers were in the beginning. I didn't want that to happen to us.

Our unit's Training NCO, Staff Sergeant Baker, was one of the soldiers who came down the week before. He was an active duty soldier who was assigned to our unit. He wasn't deploying with us but was coordinating everything for our deployment. That night, he came by our barracks. He had just found out what our mission was. He said we had been designated an FIDUW unit (Foreign Interior Defense Unconventional Warfare) and assigned to the 20th Special Forces Group. The 20th Group was a National Guard Special Forces unit (Green Berets) from Alabama. Our unit was now the 403rd Special Operations Company 20th Special Forces Group. I couldn't believe what I just heard. The only FIDUW Civil Affairs unit in the Army was the 96th Civil Affairs Battalion. Those guys were all Green Berets; they had been through years of specialized training, preparing them to perform their mission deep inside enemy territory. Baker said it all made sense now—why the Army wouldn't tell us what the mission was, or that the soldiers the unit selected for the mission should have prior combat arms experience (Infantry, Combat Engineers, or Armor) or have law enforcement experience. They didn't want us to know ahead of time that they were going to change our designation. The Army knew that it had a very difficult mission, and they didn't have enough resources on active duty to complete the mission, plus they were also planning for the invasion of Iraq. They were going to need the 96th for that mission. So they looked to the Reserves, and our unit was picked. Baker told us that he had a meeting that day at USASOC (United States Army Special Operations Command) Headquarters. He was told our unit was selected because of the high marks we got in unit readiness. All of our soldiers were Civil Affairs qualified. We had a large number of soldiers who came from combat arms, and our unit was number one in the Brigade for physical fitness and weapons qualification. The Army had designated some other units as FIDUW, and those soldiers would be sent to Special Forces training, but that training could take up to two years, and the Army didn't have two years to wait so we were to become FIDUW without the training. Ours would be on-the-job training.

Part of me was excited; this would be an opportunity of a lifetime, to go on a mission with the Green Berets. They were the best military force in the world. Their missions were always dangerous and secretive; they operated in small teams deep inside enemy territory. Now I was going to be part of the Special Forces. The other part of me was very concerned. I was forty-four years old, I didn't have any of their specialized training, and I was going to go to the most dangerous place in the world. How was I going to survive?

Our company was organized into four teams. There were three CAT-A (Civil Affairs Team Alpha) teams; these are the teams that operate in an FOB (Forward Operating Base) and perform all Civil Military operations and work directly with the Green Berets. Then there was the CAT-B (Civil Affairs Team Bravo) team; they provided all the logistical support to the A-teams. Our B- team commander was Major Matt Kellogg. He was forty-five years old and a prison guard from upstate New York. He was a veteran of the Persian Gulf War as well as Bosnia.

The next day, our training began. We had the same schedule every day. We would get up at 6:00 A.M. and fall out for physical training. Warren was a Master Fitness Instructor, so he usually led us in calisthenics. We always finished with a two-mile run along Pope Air Force Base. Breakfast was at 8:00 A.M., and at 9:00 A.M. we would board the bus for transportation to our training site. Training would last until 4:00 P.M., then it was the ride back to our barracks. Dinner was at 5:00 P.M., and the rest of the evening we would have off. Our training went six days a week with Sundays off.

Our trainers called our training familiarization training. We started out with first aid training and reacting to direct fire. They transported us to one of the big parade fields on the old post. It was 9:00 A.M., the temperature was already in the mid nineties, and there was no shade on the field. The trainers had us practicing splints, dressings, and the buddy carry. The trainers were unprepared for us, because they didn't have enough training aids to practice with. They told us they just found out the night before that they had to teach this class. If they had known sooner, they could have requested a building instead of being out in the middle of a parade field, and they would have more training aids. My concern that this training was going to be a waste of time came to fruition that very first day.

The second day was even worse, when we had the react to direct and indirect fire training. Again, they took us out to the parade field. We practiced walking in different formations and had to react when we heard one of the trainers yell "bang." After practicing this for a couple of hours, one of the trainers staked out on the ground with engineer tape, a simulated room. We then practiced clearing the simulated room. I couldn't believe this was the best training the Army could come up with. It was obvious the trainers had no idea what we would be facing. I couldn't understand why we didn't have soldiers training us who had just come back from deployment. They would know what to train us on based on their first-hand experience, and they could answer our questions. We all became very frustrated with the training. It seemed that the more training we did, the worse it got. One morning, they bused us out to a remote training area. We spent an hour and a half waiting for the trainers to show up. When they finally showed up, they told us they were given the wrong training area. They were totally unprepared for the training. They weren't sure what to go over, so the one sergeant decided to have us go over Soviet anti-tank mine recognition. Steve asked him, "What kind of antipersonnel mines might we see there?"

The sergeant stuttered and said, "You will get a briefing when you get there on the specific types of mines."

"Have you been to Afghanistan?"

"No, I haven't."

"Then how do you know that we will get that briefing?"

"Look, we were just told to go over mine recognition with you. I'm sure once you get there, they will be more specific."

"You can understand our frustration. We are headed off to a war, and this training we are getting is bullshit!"

"As I told you before, we were directed to give you this training; it is a requirement for combat certification." I pulled Steve aside and said, "I agree with you that this training is crap. The problem isn't with these two trainers; it's much higher than them. They are just doing what they are told to do. They have no idea what to train us on, because they haven't been there. We need to push these concerns up our chain of command."

"You're right; arguing with these guys is going to get us nowhere."

"I'm going to bring it up with the battalion commander, and you bring it up with Sergeant Major. It won't help us, but maybe for future deployments it will."

For the last couple of hours, we practiced crawling on our stomachs, probing for mines with our bayonets. I couldn't see myself crawling around on my belly in Afghanistan looking for mines.

The days we didn't have familiarization training were spent at the hospital getting physicals, seeing the dentist, and getting our inoculations. We had already done all this at Fort Drum so we could be ready to go if we were mobilized, but it didn't matter; it was on the checklist, so we had to do it again. The training unit had a process for every unit that was activated, and they weren't about to deviate from it.

On August 10, 2002, we finally finished all of our familiarization training and health screenings. We had a ceremony that day on the parade field certifying us ready for combat. LTC Morales gave a speech on our training accomplishments and certified us as combat ready. We were no longer under the command of the training company; we were officially attached to the 20th Special Forces Group. I thought to myself that wasn't too bad; all other Special Forces soldiers go through a grueling one and a half years of training, and we just did it in about three weeks. Later that day, I found out that my promotion to major came through. We had a small ceremony that night at the barracks, and I pinned on my new rank.

Now our focus was on when we would leave and what equipment we needed. We found out that we would be replacing three teams of the 96th Civil Affairs Battalion. Warren and I scheduled a meeting with their company commander and a couple of their soldiers who had just returned home from Afghanistan. They told us we would be operating in very remote regions with little support from our headquarters section back in Bagram. We had to become self-sufficient. After our meeting, Warren and I sat down and made a list of equipment we thought we would need. The next day, we went to the DMC (Distribution Management Center) to purchase the equipment. We were allowed to spend $50,000 on equipment. The DMC was a large store, similar to Walmart, that was run by the Army. We purchased tool sets, battery-operated saws, water purification kits, laptop computers, printers, and digital cameras. Over the next two weeks, we would be drawing all of our operational equipment and packing our Conex storage container for shipping.

I had been selected to be the purchasing agent for our team. Each team had an operational fund that the purchasing agent was to oversee. Our operational fund was $10,000. We were to use this money to pay for our interpreter and to purchase any supplies we needed from the local Afghan economy.

For the next two weeks, we were busy with drawing our equipment, getting everything packed, meeting with representatives from the 20th Group, and coordinating our flight overseas. We were all getting real sick of Fort Bragg and were eager to leave. We were finally told we would be shipping out on September 3rd. We would fly into Ramstein, Germany, and have about a week layover in Kaiserslautern, Germany. We were scheduled to leave Germany on September 11th and arrive in Afghanistan on September 12, 2002. We were given a three-day pass over Labor Day weekend, so I decided to drive home and see Lorrie and the kids one last time before we went overseas. My three days at home were terrible—it was great to see Lorrie and the kids, but I was preoccupied. Then I had to leave, we had to say our goodbyes again, and it seemed harder on everyone this time than it was in July.

5
Bagram

Our feet left American soil the morning of September 5, 2002. From Fort Bragg, we traveled to Dover Air Force Base. A C-5 cargo jet took us to a six-day layover in Ramstein, Germany. Our thoughts the entire time focused on the mission. We wanted to be in Afghanistan to start the mission. The combat tours at that time were nine months long, and our time didn't start until we landed in Afghanistan. We referred to this as our "time in the box." The sooner we got in, the sooner we could get out. Most of us had never been in combat before. The two who were veterans of the Persian Gulf War were not involved in any ground combat. Had any of us possessed any real combat experience, we would not have been so excited about getting there. I just had the stories that my father and uncles had told me. War had been glamorized—they never talked about the fear or the suffering.

Finally the day came that we were to fly to Afghanistan and start the mission. It was September 11, 2002. We had moved from Kaiserslautern to Rein Mien Air Base two days before. Our flight was scheduled to leave around 1:00 P.M. that day. There was a community room in the barracks that had a television in it. That morning, I sat and watched the one-year anniversary special on the terrorist attacks. I thought back to that day and how I wondered what my future held. I still had many of the same questions. I was about to enter a big unknown.

The flight from Germany to Afghanistan was scheduled for twelve hours. We boarded a C-17, another cargo jet smaller than the C-5. The

C-5 was too big to land in Afghanistan. All of our equipment was stored in the center of the jet, and we sat in cargo seats along the sides of the plane. At 3:00 P.M., we took off. Once we were in flight, we were able to get up and move around. There wasn't much room, with all the equipment that we were taking. I grabbed my poncho liner and crawled up on top of a Conex and tried to get some sleep. I dozed on and off, but mostly I thought about Lorrie and the kids. I replayed in my mind our last trip to Gettysburg. I wondered what they were doing now, and I thought about what lay ahead.

Finally, the pilot came on and told us we were about to enter Afghanistan airspace. He said we had to get back into our seats and buckle up, as it was going to be a rough ride. He had to make a series of evasive maneuvers to avoid being shot at. He told us we would be going in blackout, and he would be shutting all the lights off; we couldn't turn any flashlights on during that time. The lights went off and for about ten minutes. It was a quiet flight until, all of a sudden, the plane pitched violently to the left then to the right. We no sooner had leveled out when we started in a steep dive. Our ears were popping. I grabbed ahold of the cargo strap, and the plane leveled out again. Finally, I heard the landing gear engage, and we were on the ground. The pilot came on and welcomed us to Bagram Air Base Afghanistan.

We gathered up our gear, and the loading ramp came down. I walked down the ramp and, as I exited the airplane, I was hit with a blast of heat. The pilot told us the air temperature was a balmy 115 degrees. I had never felt heat like this before. I felt the sweat start running down the middle of my back. I looked around, and I could immediately tell I was in a war zone. Parked along the tarmac were Apache attack helicopters, and on the northern end of the runway there were several destroyed Soviet MIG fighters. The buildings surrounding the airfield showed the scars of war. They were full of bullet holes; some had gaping holes in them from a tank or RPG (Rocket Propelled Grenade) round.

We were met by Sergeant Thompson, a member of the 96th Civil Affairs, the unit we were replacing. He was going to take us to the in-processing building and then over to the CJSOTF (Combined Joint Special Operations Task Force) compound where we would be staying until the teams moved out to the firebases. Warren and I got our team together at the front of the airplane; we briefed them on what was going on. I said, "Let's get a team picture of our first few minutes in

Afghanistan," so we lined up on the tarmac and had our picture taken. The other teams liked that idea, and they did the same thing.

We moved from the tarmac to the in-processing building where we had to sign in and receive a briefing. The in-processing sergeant gave us the briefing and showed us a layout of Bagram Air Base. There were several Multi National Forces stationed at Bagram, along with the United States personnel. There were contingencies from Great Brittan, Italy, Germany, Canada, and South Korea. They all had their own camps at Bagram. The sergeant gave us a history of Bagram. He told us it was originally a Soviet air base and, during their control of the base, they put several thousand land mines around the base to protect it. When they pulled out, they put several thousand more throughout the base. Most of the mines on the populated part of the base had been recovered, but if we were going out to the outer edges of the base, we needed to make sure we stayed on the road, as those areas of the base had not been cleared yet. Several areas outside the base and along the road to Kabul had been mined. He showed us how to identify where the minefields were.

At the end of the briefing, Sergeant Thompson led us to our compound. It seemed like a long walk, but really it was only about a half mile. I was extremely hot and thirsty, and I hadn't had much sleep in the last two days. We finally got to our compound, Sergeant Thompson showed the guards at the gate his identification, and they let us in. The compound was filled with row after row of tents. They were the old, general-purpose, medium green canvas tents that the Army has been using for the last sixty years.

As we walked through the compound to our area, we would get stares and snickers from the soldiers there. It reminded me of a scene from the movie, *Platoon,* when Charlie Sheen got off the airplane in Viet Nam and he was getting dirty looks from the soldiers who had been there for a long time and were getting ready to leave. These guys who were looking at us had a different look about themselves. They all had beards, their faces had a weathered look, and they had a haunted stare. They were wearing baseball caps. Their DCUs (Desert Combat Uniforms) were completely blank, with no unit patches, no qualification badges, no rank, and no name tapes. We obviously looked like virgin soldiers. Our uniforms were brand new, and we had our unit patches, rank, name, and U.S. Army tapes still sewn on.

We finally got to an empty tent where one of the teams would stay. I walked in, and it must have been twenty degrees hotter in there than it was outside. There were six cots inside, and everything was covered in dust and sand. I couldn't believe the conditions we were going to live in. One of the other teams decided to take that tent. Only one other tent was available. and our Bravo team took that one. Our team and the other remaining team, twelve of us in all, were taken over to a small storage building next to the supply building. We could barley fit twelve cots and our gear in there. It was stifling hot, and the air was so thick you could cut it with a knife. I sat on the cot and thought to myself, "How am I ever going to survive this?" It had been a long time since I was in the Infantry and had lived in such conditions. I had become pretty pampered. I was used to sleeping in a nice, soft bed. When it was hot, I would turn on the air conditioning, and if I was thirsty, I went to the refrigerator and got a drink. I wasn't the hard charger that I used to be, going on twenty-mile road marches with a sixty-pound rucksack on my back, with little sleep. I used to thrive on that kind of training, but not anymore.

I remembered back to my first day of boot camp; the drill sergeants were in my face yelling at me, making me do push-ups in that hot New Jersey sun. I didn't think I could make it through boot camp, but I did, and I was an honor graduate. I had to summon up the will to survive and the determination to succeed that was inside me. This time it wasn't just about me; I had six other soldiers who would look to me for leadership and guidance. It was my responsibility that we perform our mission and return home safely.

Thompson said he would be back in about an hour and take us over to the chow hall. Then, at 7:00 P.M., we had a mandatory briefing in the JOC (Joint Operations Center) where we would meet the commander of the 20th Special Forces Group and have a briefing on the rules of engagement.

As I got my area situated and as comfortable as I could make it, I could hear the wind outside really howling. I walked out, and there was a sandstorm. The wind was really strong, and it was blowing sand and dirt into our room. I could hear all the tents rattling. We were told that this happens every night about this time. Bagram was surrounded by mountains from the Hindu Kush mountain range. As the temperature dropped, the mountains created this windstorm every night that lasted about two hours and, of course, the wind picked up all the sand and blew it everywhere. That was why everything had a coating of sand and dirt on it.

Our briefing that night was given to us by the 20th Group's JAG (Judge Advocate General) officer. The rules of engagement were that if we came under fire from a hostile force, we had the right to use deadly physical force, and if any civilian's life was endangered by a hostile force, deadly physical force was authorized. Taliban and Al-Qaeda forces did not wear uniforms, so our enemy could be anybody. Many of the Taliban and Al-Qaeda had escaped to Pakistan, where they had a safe haven. If we were taking fire from an enemy position located within Pakistan, we could return fire, but we were not allowed to cross the border and go after the enemy forces.

Warlords governed each Afghanistan province. These warlords had their own armies; they had all been high-ranking Taliban leaders. These warlords were providing weapons and security to Al-Qaeda. The main focus where we would be operating was to capture these warlords, seize their weapons caches, and dismantle their armies. After the JAG's briefing, the commander of the 20th group, Colonel Stratton, came in and welcomed us. He told us we would be OPCON (Operationally Connected) to a Special Forces A-team and support them with whatever CMO they needed (Civil Military Operations). Hamid Karzai was now the Interim President of Afghanistan, and his three goals were to build roads, drill water wells for each village to provide clean and safe water, and to build schools. The colonel told us that, too, would be part of our mission—to designate water wells for the villages, build as many schools as possible, and provide humanitarian relief in our area of operation. Our job was to win the hearts and minds of the locals, which in turn would make it easier to hunt down Al-Qaeda.

Our briefing ended about 9:00 P.M., and we made our way back to our "hooch" (Army slang for living quarters). As I lay on my cot and reflected on the day, I knew what our mission was, and I knew who the enemy was but I didn't know what he looked like, and I didn't know where he was. My father and my uncles knew who their enemies were—they were the Germans and the Japanese. They wore uniforms, and there were clearly defined lines: the enemy was to their front. I could see that my war was going to be much different from the one they fought.

The next day, Sergeant Thompson took us over to the supply building to get our body armor. These were much better than the old flack vests. These were made of Kevlar, and a steel plate was inserted in the center of the vest for additional protection. Then we were issued our cargo vests, which carried all of our M-16 magazines and hand grenades. We wore these vests over our body armor. The only problem with this type of vest was it was bulky and heavy—much heavier than the vest I wore in the police department. After everyone got their gear,

Thompson told me he was going to take me over to the communications center and get me a satellite phone. He said that would be the most critical piece of equipment I would have. He said sometimes the radios don't work, and if we come under fire and we can't radio for help, we will have to use the phone to call back to Bagram for help. He said he had to use the phone many times. The only problem was they were short of phones, so he wanted to get me over there as soon as possible. I was lucky the communications center had one satellite phone left, and I got it.

There were three Forward Operating Bases, or firebases as we called them, from which our teams were to operate. These were Firebase Asadabad, fifty miles west of Bagram in the Kunar Province; Firebase Orgun, 120 miles southeast of Bagram in Paktia Province; and Firebase Lwara, 140 miles southeast of Bagram in Paktia Province and about one and a half miles west of the Pakistan border. Firebase Lwara was the hot spot of the three. With its close proximity to the Pakistan border, it was a target for Taliban and Al-Qaeda forces operating out of Pakistan. The firebase was subject to ambushes and rocket and mortar attacks on a weekly basis. At the time, it was considered the most dangerous place in the world. The decision was made to send our team to Lwara; Matt thought that, with the experience in law enforcement that our team had, we had the best chance of survival in that hostile environment.

That night, we had a briefing of the Lwara AO (Area of Operation). We were told that it was a mountainous, harsh, arid terrain at an average of eight thousand feet above sea level. It had fifteen inches of rainfall annually; however, for the past five years, the area had been plagued by drought. The valleys were collection points for rain and snow melt, which had formed dry riverbeds. There were no roads other than the dry riverbeds. The steep terrain on both sides of the riverbeds favored enemy activity. There was no formal Afghan government in the region. There were only two local tribes, the Pepoli and the Gayan. These tribes were heavily influenced by the Taliban. Firebase Lwara was located within the Pepoli tribal area. To date, forty-four rocket attacks had occurred on the firebase, and eleven ambushes on U.S. personnel since the firebase inception sixty days before. The Gayan tribal region has been identified with Taliban flags flying on about forty percent of the houses. The local populace's mood was aggressive and resentful.

After the briefing, we sat down with Thompson, it was his team that we were replacing at Lwara. He had been there since they started the firebase two months before. He told us that many Afghans in the Lwara AO were suffering from malaria, typhoid fever, and tuberculosis; we had to be very careful when we were dealing with these people. There were no hospitals in the area, and only a couple of doctors with very limited supplies. These people will come to the firebase to seek treatment. He also told us that they have hired locals to work at the firebase, but the enemy has informants in the firebase workforce. Radio communications indicate that U.S. forces are being monitored and reported to a higher command. He told us that we had to be very careful when around the workers. Enemy informants understand English, so we could not talk about any military operations when they were around. He said it had been very difficult to perform any Civil Affairs missions due to the hostility of the area. Most of the time, his CAT-A team had been assisting the Special Forces A-team with combat operations. It was obvious this was going to be a very difficult and dangerous mission.

Each firebase received a resupply each week; Lwara's resupply was scheduled for September 17th, and we would be airlifted into Lwara then. The next four days were spent going through our Conex and packing everything we wanted to take with us. We would be flying in on a Chinook helicopter, so we had a limited amount of space; what we didn't take with us now, we would request that our B team send on a resupply.

6
Lwara

September 17th finally arrived. We had spent a long four days waiting to ship out. I spent time picking Sergeant Thompson's brain. He knew what we were in for, so he tried to give us as much information as he could to prepare us. The plan was that, once we got to Lwara, we would spend about two weeks transitioning; they called it "left seat, right seat." The first week, we would be observers (the right seat), and the 96th would take the lead on the missions. We would assist when needed. The second week, we would take the lead (left seat), and they would be the observers, helping out when needed. Thompson said they would take us to all nine villages in the AO; some of the villages were friendly, but others were very dangerous. One of the most hostile places was the village of Gayan; this was home to Bakka Jan, a local warlord and ranking member of the Taliban. It was suspected that he was the one coordinating the attacks on the firebase and the ambushes on U.S. personnel.

We boarded the Chinook helicopter for the twenty-five-minute ride from Bagram to Lwara. This being a resupply mission, we were limited as to what we could take with us. There were two Chinooks along with an Apache gunship that flew security. My heart raced as the Chinook powered up; the deafening roar of the helicopters' blades going faster and faster, we hovered for a few seconds, then off we went. The rear door was down. The crew chief sat on it with his feet hanging off, holding the 240-Bravo machine gun. His head moved back and forth as he scanned the mountain ridges. As we flew, we hugged the sides of the mountains. I could look out the side window and see what appeared to be compounds scattered across the valley floor. They reminded me of the old western movie, "Fort Apache." These compounds were square, with tall walls; they were the same color as the ground, so they must have been made of earth. As I would later find out, these were the Afghans' houses. They built their houses with these tall walls to protect themselves from thieves and invaders.

As the helicopters landed on the LZ (Landing Zone), they kicked up an enormous dust cloud. As soon as we touched down, there was a scurry of activity: the crew chief started tossing bags out of the helicopter, other soldiers on the ground ran into the helicopter and started pulling the gear off, and the crew chief was yelling to hurry up and get the gear off. I grabbed as much as I could and jumped off the helicopter. As I looked around, several vehicles were racing up to us; as soon as they got to us, we started throwing the equipment on them. There was a definite urgency to what everyone was doing. As we unloaded, the Apache was flying around the surrounding hilltops providing cover, and I could see Humvee gunships (Humvees with fifty caliber machine guns or Mark 19 automatic grenade launchers mounted on top) placed strategically around the LZ. The helicopters were on the ground a total of three minutes, and as soon as everything was unloaded, they powered up and took off.

Thompson came up to me and said, "We have to get everything loaded and get the hell out of here, this is a hot LZ." I didn't know it, but as we were landing, we were engaged by some small arms fire to our north. As soon as Thompson said that to me, I could hear the distinct sound of a .50 caliber machine gun, with its methodical pop, pop, pop, being fired. One of the security elements on the north side of the LZ was returning fire. We got our equipment on the vehicles and headed up to the firebase.

On the eastern side of the LZ, on top of a hill, sat the firebase. The firebase was flanked by large mountains to the east. These mountains represented the border between Afghanistan and Pakistan. During the 1800s through the early 1900s, Afghanistan found itself the center of competing powers—England to its east in India, and Russia to its north in Turkistan. The British repeatedly carried out incursions into Afghanistan for both commercial reasons and geopolitical goals. Three conflicts ensued between England and Afghanistan, culminating in the Treaty of Rawalpindi on August 19, 1919, granting independence to Afghanistan. The treaty left one of the most significant marks on the country, the drawing of Afghanistan's modern boundary. The British separated Pakistan from Afghanistan's border exclusively on slopes so that military units approaching Afghanistan would have a superior position, firing down upon the Afghans during a conflict. This border was known as the Durand Line. The firebase was a mile and a half from the Durand Line. Taliban and Al-Qaeda forces repeatedly used this line to their advantage by carrying out rocket and mortar attacks on the firebase.

It was a short but steep ride up to the firebase. It was a large compound like the ones I saw from the helicopter. Inside the compound were six tents that housed two Special Forces teams from the 7th Special Forces Group, ODA-762, and ODA-765, and a SOT-A team (Special Operations Tactic Team) from the 20th Special Forces Group. The operations center was housed in a small building along an inside wall of the compound. On the backside of the compound, outside the walls, were the tents for a rifle platoon and mortar section from the 82nd Airborne Division, and the 96th Civil Affairs team. The 82nd provided the base security along with a QRF (Quick Reactionary Force). If a unit came under attack outside the firebase, the QRF would respond.

There were two observation posts, one in the front of the compound, manned by two soldiers and armed with the 240-Bravo machine gun, and an observation tower at the back of the compound with the same configuration. There were bunkered fighting positions scattered around the back of the compound. The mortar pit, with two eighty-one-mm mortars, was located in the center of the 82nd's area. On the roof of the operations center was the FLIR (Forward Looking Infrared Radar). Surrounding the back of the compound were Hesco Barriers. These barriers have converted the traditional sandbag walling concept into an enhanced Blast Wall System. The barriers are four feet tall by four feet wide and filled with sand and stones. Outside the back gate was home to the AMF (Afghan Military Forces). The AMF were former members of Bakka Jan's Army, but they now worked for the United States. They provided a rear security element for the firebase. There were about ten soldiers in the AMF; the 7th Group paid for their services.

We unloaded our gear, and Thompson took us over to his tent to meet the rest of his team, Staff Sergeant Burke and Sergeant Riddell. He told us they were turning their tent over to us and they would bunk with one of the SF teams. The tent was the same type that was in Bagram. It was hot and dusty, with eight cots and a table. It was 12:30

P.M. and we were all hungry, so he took us down to the chow tent located in front of the compound. He told us it was MREs (Meals Ready to Eat) for breakfast and lunch, and hot T-Rats (Tray Pack Rations, meals heated in the container) for dinner. We grabbed an MRE and went back to our tent. Thompson gave us a rundown on the operations of the base. The only base duty that we would have was the radio room. Our team would be responsible for a four-hour shift a couple times a week.

They hired locals to do the day-to-day work—fixing the walls from the attacks, filling the Hesco Barriers, burning the waste from the latrine, baking bread, and doing the laundry. He told us the first thing we needed to do was "sterilize" our uniforms. We had to remove all of our name tapes, unit patches, and rank. We never used anybody's last name or rank—it was first name only. Whenever we received mail, we were required to burn everything with our names or addresses. We never talked about operations when we were around the workers. They caught a worker one day measuring in paces the length of the rear of the compound; they found out he was working for Bakka Jan.

Burke gave us a tour of the bunkers and fighting positions. When the base comes under attack, we man the fighting positions on the west side. Burke told us that tonight they would run a drill so we could become familiar with what to do during an attack. We spent a couple of hours getting settled in. Warren and I went over to the operations center and met with the team leaders for the 7th group. They weren't very happy to see us. Captain Tom Brady, the team leader for 762, said, "So you guys are the reservists. Hope you got your heads on straight. The shit happens here fast, and I don't have time to babysit anyone." I told him not to worry, we can handle what ever is thrown at us. Captain Mitch Ross was the team leader for 765; he introduced himself then asked us what we did in civilian life. Warren told him he was a teacher, and I told him I was a school administrator and retired police officer. Brady perked up and said, "You were a cop?" I told him about the time I spent in law enforcement. Brady said his brother was a police officer in Fort Worth, Texas, and when his Army tour was up, he wanted to get into law enforcement, too. I told him one of our other team members, Steve, was a police officer for the Syracuse Police Department. Brady said, "No kidding, that's great." We sat and talked for awhile, it turned out to be a real good meeting; they felt much more comfortable with us since they knew our backgrounds. Steve and Roger met with the team sergeants, and Steve hit it off with them. They found out he was a police officer, and that gave them a lot more confidence in us. Steve had an easygoing personality. Once you met him, it seemed like you had known him all your life. The SF (Special Forces) team sergeants really liked him, which made things a lot easier for our team.

Each unit at the firebase had its own interpreter. The 96th had an interpreter, but he decided to go back to Kabul and work for the U.S. Embassy. Thompson found someone who was interested. His name was Naime Jan. One of the other interpreters at the firebase knew him and recommended him to Thompson. He was from Khost, a village forty miles north of Lwara. Naime was twenty-three years old; his parents fled to Pakistan during the Russian occupation. It was in Pakistan that he learned to speak English. He returned to Afghanistan after the U.S. invasion to find work as an interpreter. That night, he came by our tent to meet with us. Naime's English was every bit as good as ours, and he was familiar with the AO. Everyone on the team liked him, so we hired him. The interpreters lived on the firebase, and they were paid $200 per week. This was more money than the average Afghan made in a year.

Our first mission was the following day, so Naime needed to get ready for it. One of the other interpreters took Naime out to the AMF where they issued him an AK-47 and cargo vest. All interpreters were armed with an AK-47; they had the same rules of engagement. During this mission, we were going to meet with a doctor then take a trip to the northern end of the AO and visit the village of Wrice. Anytime we left the firebase, we had to send a Conop (Convoy Operation) to the CJSOTF in Bagram. We went over the procedure with Thompson, and then we got together with representatives from the 82nd and 7th groups to discuss the mission. The 82nd provided a security element on any mission that went outside the wire. The 7th Group replaced the 3rd Special Forces Group the week prior to our arrival. They had not been to the northern part of the AO yet, so they would be accompanying us. Brady said the SOT-A team got some radio intercepts last night about an attack on a U.S. base. They couldn't tell what base or what kind of attack, and intelligence reports stated that the village of Wrice was a hotbed of Taliban activity. We had to be ready for anything.

The last thing we did that night before we turned in was to conduct the drill. The FLIR was manned from 6:00 P.M. to 6:00 A.M. every day. In the event of an attack, the person manning the FLIR would sound an air horn then yell "incoming," referring to a rocket or mortar round that had been fired at the firebase and telling us to take cover.

Thompson had briefed us earlier on actions to take during an attack. At 8:30 P.M., the air horn sounded; we put on our body armor and Kevlar helmets, grabbed our weapons, and hopped into our bunker. We had the three fighting positions on the west side of the firebase; two of us manned each position. Once everyone had taken up a fighting position, the mortar section fired two illumination flares. When the flares burned out, the "all clear" was given, and the drill was over. We moved back to our tent and went over what had been done. I thought it went pretty well. Although it was dark, and we were not allowed to have any white lights on outside our tents, the moon was very bright, and we were able to find the bunker and take up a fighting position with out any trouble.

It had been a very busy day, and I was on a steep learning curve; there was a lot to learn, and we had a lot to prove. Overall, I thought it was a good day, and the next day we would be going on our first mission outside the wire.

7

Baptism under Fire

Warren was an early riser. Our bunks were right next to each other, and by 5:00 A.M., he was ready to go. I didn't sleep very well the night before, so I decided to get up early, too. We walked down to the chow tent and got a cup of coffee. We sat there and talked about how things were going to run. We decided that on all combat operations, I would take the lead; on the humanitarian missions, Warren would take the lead. I had the infantry experience, and with my experience in law enforcement, Warren thought I was better prepared to lead the team during combat operations. I was glad Warren wanted to do that, for I was confident in my infantry skills; I think Warren saw how well I hit it off with Brady, and it would be easier for me to do the planning with them than it would be for him. I told Warren that Steve would be my Team Sergeant when I was running the missions. Steve and I had talked about our time as police officers and swapped a lot of war stories. He had a lot of the same experiences I had, and even more. Steve had the respect of the other members of the team; he was a strong NCO (Non-Commissioned Officer).

We went back to the tent and got the rest of the team up. Thompson came over to our tent with the Platoon Leader and Platoon Sergeant for the 82nd, Lieutenant Mark Stevens and Sergeant First Class Ron Spycher. Stevens was twenty-three years old and fresh out of college. SFC Spycher had eighteen years in the military and was a veteran of Panama and the Persian Gulf War. The funny thing about Spycher was that he had been Tim's drill sergeant when Tim was in basic training. When Spycher walked into our tent that morning, Tim didn't know what to do. During basic training, when a drill sergeant walks into your room, you jump up and assume the position of parade rest. Tim saw him and immediately jumped up and went to parade rest. We all started laughing. Spycher told Tim to relax, he wasn't in basic training anymore, and for Tim to call him Ron. Tim laughed, but you could tell he was uneasy around him. Lieutenant Stevens said they would be providing a security element for us today; he had two gunships and ten soldiers. SFC Spycher would be the NCOIC (Non-Commissioned Officer in Charge) for the 82nd on our mission today. Thompson told us to make sure we pack enough gear in case we can't make it back to the firebase that night. We needed an extra uniform and boots, three MREs, spare batteries, and extra ammunition—he called it a "go bag." Warren, Thompson, and I went over to the operation center and met with Captain Ross. He and four of his team members would be going with us, and they would be taking a gunship. Brady was going to stay back at the firebase. Thompson and Burke would be going along with all of us.

At 9:30 A.M., we met at the front of the compound. Captain Ross went over the mission and, in the event of an ambush, what actions we needed to take. We pulled out of the firebase at 10:15 A.M. and headed to the firing range to test fire the weapons. The range was located on the northern end of the LZ. We fired our rifles, and the gunships fired their .50 caliber and Mark 19 grenade launcher. We wanted to make sure that all of our weapons were functioning properly. After all the weapons were test fired we headed out, two gunships in the lead, and then our two Mercedes were followed by two more gunships. We headed east toward Pakistan. Dr. Nikeeb was the local doctor whom we were going to visit first. He was from Pakistan but moved across the border six months ago. He ran a small clinic adjacent to his compound.

We followed a dry riverbed that wound its way along the valley. Jagged rocks, stones, and sand covered the ground with some low, thorny shrubs scattered around, and an occasional juniper tree. It was a fifteen-minute drive from the firebase to the doctor's compound. On arrival, the four gunships took up a defensive position guarding both the east and west approach. Sergeant Spycher placed his soldiers in defensive positions around the perimeter of the compound. Steve had Tim and Fred assist with the perimeter security. Spycher thought he saw some movement on the mountain behind the compound; he used the scope mounted on his M-4 rifle to scan the side of the mountain. There was a trail that ran along the side of the mountain; Spycher told his soldiers to watch that trail. The mountain was in Pakistan. It looked over the firebase, and it was a favorite spot for the Taliban to fire rockets at the firebase.

Warren, Steve, Thompson, and I, along with Ross, two of his team members, Sergeant First Class Mike Mauldin, weapons specialist, Staff Sergeant Gary Richards, demolitions expert, and Naime, met with the doctor. The doctor had visited the firebase before, so Thompson knew him, and he introduced us. Our mission was twofold; the doctor was interested in starting a school, and he needed medicine for his clinic. We were going to talk to him about his school plans and see what medicines he needed. Ross had information that the doctor was a member of the Taliban and instrumental in the recent attacks on the firebase. An informant told Ross the reason he opened a clinic where he did was to keep an eye on the Americans, not to treat the sick. Ross wasn't sure if he was a real doctor. Ross and his team wanted to find evidence that supported this information. The doctor was very happy to meet us. He immediately wanted us to sit and have chi with him. It was a custom in Afghanistan to serve chi to your guest. In this part of Afghanistan, chi is made with black tea, goat's milk, and sugar. The doctor motioned to one of his workers to get the chi. He had another worker bring out a mat for us to sit on. The eight of us and the doctor sat in a circle on the mat in front of his clinic and drank chi. I was a little concerned about whether it was safe to drink. Thompson and Ross were drinking it, so I decided it must be all right.

Warren asked the doctor about the school he wanted to build. He said he wanted to build a school for boys. Naime looked over to me and said, "He wants to build a Madrasah." A Madrasah was an Islamic fundamentalist school; only boys were allowed to attend. These schools were sponsored by the Taliban. President Karzai had outlawed Madrasahs. Warren told him that we would like to build a school in the Lwara valley, but it must be open to both boys and girls.

As Warren talked to the doctor about the school and clinic, I could tell he was hiding something. As a police officer, I had interviewed many people who had committed crimes. I could tell when people were lying or trying to hide something; their body language would always give them away. As Warren talked to the doctor about the clinic, he was very fidgety; he had a string of beads in his hand that he kept rubbing. He wouldn't make eye contact with Warren; every time Warren asked him a question, he would look to the ground when he answered. Steve was sitting next to me, and I leaned over to him and asked him what he thought of the doctor. Steve said, "He's full of shit, look how he's acting."

"I know, he won't even look at Warren when answering him."

Then Steve said, "Who the fuck are these guys over here looking at us? They don't look like fuckin' nurses." I motioned to Ross; I wanted him to look at the doctor's two helpers. They looked like they were up to no good; Steve thought the same thing. I couldn't tell from where I was sitting, but it looked like they were whispering to each other and kicking the sand around. We finished our chi, and Warren and Thompson went with the doctor to see the clinic. I was more interested in what the doctor's two helpers were up to. Steve and I, along with Ross, Mauldin, and Richards, looked around outside. Ross wanted to find anything that could be used to fire the rockets: wire, batteries, or fuses. Richards found some batteries in the dirt behind the compound. Now I knew what the doctor's two helpers were up to. Ross told Naime to ask the doctor what he was doing with the batteries. Dr. Nikeeb said he used them for his radio; he must have dropped them when he was out back. The doctor was real nervous when he answered. Steve looked over to Ross and said, "This guy is one big bullshitter."

Naime looked at me and said, "Sir I do not think he is telling the truth."

"Good call, Naime; I don't think he is either," I replied. Warren told the doctor he wanted to meet with him again and that he was going to check with Bagram to see if he could help get him some medicine for his clinic. I thought to myself there was no way I wanted to help him. There was no doubt in my mind that he had bad intentions. Ross motioned to his watch; it was time for us to leave. We thanked him for the chi and got back into our vehicles and left. As we were driving out, Thompson looked over to me and said, "He's dirty. I know he's involved in the rocket attacks."

"He sure is. He was lying to us the whole time. Did you see how nervous he was when Richards found those batteries?"

"Don't trust him, and don't give him anything."

"I agree. I will talk with Warren and let him know what we saw." I knew that Warren was eager to start a humanitarian project, and we all wanted to. Warren didn't see things the way Steve and I did; Steve and I had been around burglars, rapists, and murderers. We knew what the criminal mind was like; if we didn't know someone, we didn't trust them. Warren didn't have the experience in dealing with that devious part of society. He always saw the good in everyone. In this part of the world, when dealing with these people, you had to expect the worst; trusting the wrong person could get you killed.

Wrice was about an hour's drive north. We were about fifteen minutes into our trip when the rear gunship called and said, "We've got company." We were being followed by two vehicles; they were about fifteen hundred to two thousand yards to our east, just over the Pakistan border. Spycher was in the rear vehicle. He said he spotted them a few minutes after we left Dr. Nikeeb's clinic and they had been with us ever since. We stopped the vehicles and got into a defensive position. Mauldin trained the binoculars on them; he could see that one vehicle appeared to be a dark-colored sport utility vehicle. He couldn't tell how many were in the vehicle. The second was a small pickup truck with three or four individuals in the back. It was lunchtime, so Ross decided to take a break and eat an MRE while we kept an eye on the two vehicles. They were definitely keeping an eye on us, because they stopped too. We stayed there for about twenty minutes then took off for Wrice. We started heading northwest. The vehicles that were following us never crossed the border, and we finally lost them. The whole situation made us nervous and edgy.

We pulled into Wrice around 2:30 P.M. It was a small village with a population of approximately eight hundred residents. As we drove through the village, Thompson said, "Something is wrong. Usually, when we pull into a village, kids come running up to the vehicle for a handout. It's never this quiet." The lead gunship called on the radio and said they spotted a guy on the roof signaling with a mirror. "They knew we were coming."

"Do you think those vehicles that were following us had something to do with this?" I asked.

"Could be. I've got a bad feeling."

Ross radioed, "Take a look at your nine o'clock." The village mosque was flying a Taliban flag, but President Karzai had outlawed Taliban flags.

"I've seen enough, let's get the hell out of here."

Thompson looked at me and said, "That's good, I'm a short-timer. I don't need any more problems. When we send in our SITREP (Situation Report) tonight. we need to advise Bagram that Wrice has Taliban flags flying."

We made it back to the firebase around 4:00 P.M. We unloaded our gear and headed over to the operations center for an AAR (After Action Review). We discussed the mission—what went well and what didn't. Ross thought it went well; our trip to the doctor's clinic reinforced his belief that the doctor is involved in the attacks on the base. After the AAR, we went over the next day's mission to Gayan. When we finished up, it was time to eat, and we went to the chow tent. After dinner, we went back to our tent. Tim brought with him three hundred movies on DVD. That night, we picked out a movie, and we sat around our laptop computer and watched it. Naime loved to watch American movies, so we invited him to stay and watch. Naime was fitting right in with our team. We finished the movie at 10:00 P.M.; I was dead tired—all of us were. I knew tonight I would get a good night's sleep. We turned out the lights and hit the sack.

"INCOMING, INCOMING, INCOMING," a soldier yelled. The air horn blasted. I was sound asleep. I sat up dazed. I wasn't sure where I was, then all of a sudden there was a flash of light and a tremendous explosion. Stones and debris were hurled against the tent. The concussion from the blast knocked me out of my cot. I realized we were under attack, and the rocket must have hit close to the tent. I knew we had to get out of the tent and into the bunker. Warren was knocked out of his bunk by the blast, too, and fell on top of me. I pushed him off and yelled to everyone to get to the bunker. Where was my gear? I couldn't find anything. Warren was trying to find his gear but couldn't. Thompson told us to make sure we put everything where we could find it. I thought I did, but it was dark, and I couldn't find my helmet or boots.

"INCOMING, INCOMING, INCOMING," a loud roar went over the top of the tent. I had never heard anything like that before, and then there was another flash and explosion. It sounded like it landed in the LZ. I finally found my helmet and vest. I put them on, and I grabbed a rifle. I couldn't find my boots. Everyone in the tent was scrambling.

Another soldier yelled, "INCOMING, INCOMING, INCOMING."

I was just outside the tent, someone yelled, "GET DOWN, GET DOWN," then there was a flash and another explosion. This one hit the Hesco Barrier on the east side. My ears were ringing so badly I could barely hear. I jumped up and ran for the bunker.

I dove in just in time to hear, "INCOMING, INCOMING, INCOMING." I heard the loud roar just above the bunker. Another foot lower, and it would have hit it. The rocket landed in the LZ. The soldier operating the FLIR had a fix on the position from which the rockets were being launched—the mountain directly east of the firebase. I sat up in the bunker and looked around; Roger and Tim were in the bunker with me. I peered out the bunker toward the mountain. The spot from which they were launching the rockets was directly at my twelve o'clock. My bunker was completely open on that side. The bunker was designed to defend an attack coming from the west; it was well fortified from that direction. But this attack was coming from the east. I had no protection from that side. If the rocket fired from that side hit our bunker, we would be killed. As I was looking at the mountain, I saw a flash. Another rocket was launched. "INCOMING, INCOMING, INCOMING." I tried to bury myself as far down in the ground as I could, but I knew it wouldn't do any good if the rocket hit the bunker. I thought to myself that this was going to be it, then I heard the roar again. This time it was even louder. It skimmed over the top of the bunker then hit the LZ with an explosion. I felt completely helpless; I couldn't shoot back. All I could do was lie there and hope it didn't hit me.

Just then the mortar section ran to the mortar tubes. The soldier on the FLIR started yelling out coordinates to the mortar sergeant. He put the coordinates into his mortar ballistic computer. Seconds later, he was giving them the deflection, elevation, and charge. Then "Whump, Whump, Whump," rounds downrange. Seconds later, the mountainside exploded in a series of deafening fireballs. As soon as the first three rounds impacted, the FLIR gave them the coordinates to adjust their fire. They made the adjustment then fired two more rounds. When those two rounds hit, the FLIR soldier yelled, "Fire for effect!" The mortars then fired a volley of ten rounds. It was a sight to see. That mortar sergeant worked those tubes like a conductor works a fine symphony.

When the volley was over, we waited. It was dead quiet, the attack was over, and the all-clear sign was given. I couldn't believe what I just went through. I had never been so scared in all my life. All the dangerous situations I experienced in the police department paled in comparison to this. My head was pounding, my ears were ringing so bad I could barely hear anything, and I wrenched my back when I jumped into the bunker. I checked with Tim and Roger; they were all right, but their ears were ringing too. Steve, Warren, and Fred made it to their bunker, and they were fine—a little shaken up, but fine. A couple guys from the 82nd got minor shrapnel wounds, but nothing serious. The medic patched them up. It was amazing no one was seriously injured or killed.

They fired five rockets at us. Two of the Hesco Barriers took a direct hit, and the other three landed in the LZ. Thompson came over and checked on us. He said, "Welcome to Afghanistan, you just earned your CIB" (Combat Infantryman Badge). The CIB is awarded to an infantryman who has received direct or indirect fire from enemy forces. To an infantryman, it is the most coveted badge you can earn, and then I knew why. One thing I knew, I was going to sandbag the opening to that bunker to protect it from attacks from the east. We gathered up our stuff and made it back to the tent. None of us was prepared for that. I thought I was ready after the drill the day before, but I wasn't. I now knew the importance of knowing where your equipment was. We only had a few seconds to get out of the tent and get in the bunker. I rearranged everything so it would be easier to find. I lay back down, but I couldn't get back to sleep for quite some time. I kept replaying over in my mind what happened and what my chances of surviving this for nine months were.

The morning after the attack, I decided to call home. The Army authorized us one ten-minute phone call home per week with the satellite phone. We were not allowed to talk about military operations or divulge our location. The Army was very serious about OPSEC (Operational Security). If we were caught violating OPSEC, we could be relieved of command or even subject to court martial. Lorrie already knew where I was. When I was in Bagram, I wrote her a letter and told her we were going to Firebase Lwara. Anytime something happened, the Army would issue a press release from Bagram, and Lorrie would go online and read about it on the Department of Defense news. It was good to hear her voice; I wasn't sure the night before if I was going to get a chance to hear it again. It was really hard not to talk about what I was doing, so it was a one-sided conversation. The only thing I told her was I was busy; she could tell by the sound of my voice it was not a good busy. I talked to the boys for a couple of minutes, and they told me what was going on in school. The ten minutes went by fast, and it was always hard to say goodbye.

Warren and I headed over to the Op center for our briefing on the day's mission. Thompson was already there along with Brady, Stevens, and Spycher. Brady said he would be going on the mission today. Thompson asked, "Did you get any sleep after the attack last night?"

"Not much," I said. Warren and Steve said they didn't get much either. "You'll get used to it."

Ross walked in and heard us talking about the attack. He said, "It's real funny how we went and visited him during the day then got rocketed at night."

"The good doctor came to the firebase last week, and we talked about his school and clinic; that was the night we got rocketed," Thompson interjected.

"We'll get him, it's just a matter of time," Brady said.

Gayan was an hour south of the firebase. It was the largest village in the AO, with a population of fifteen hundred people. It was also home to Bakka Jan, local warlord and a ranking member of the Taliban. Our mission today was to meet with the village elder and talk about a well proposal. In Afghanistan, a village elder is the same as a mayor in the United States. The 96th had done some preliminary work in Gayan on drilling a well, but they hadn't decided on a location. The elders always wanted the well located next to their compound. They also wanted to control everything, to include the water wells. At one time, most villages had water wells, and those wells were located close to the elders' compound. During the Russian occupation, the Russians contaminated the water in the wells, rendering them useless as they left the country, forcing the villagers to get their water from a nearby creek or river. One of President Karzai's top priorities was to provide clean, healthy water for the villages. Our goal was to place the well where it was most convenient to all the residents of the village.

The 96th was still negotiating with the elder on the placement. We were also going to visit the local bazaar. A bazaar is a general store that sells everything from food to clothes. Brady wanted to do a reconnaissance of the village and see Bakka Jan's compound. Thompson told us we should exchange some of our American money for Pakistan currency. Once a week, one of the interpreters would make a trip into Pakistan and exchange our U.S. currency for rupees, Pakistan's currency. Afghanistan had its own currency, Afghanis, but it had little value. In this area of Afghanistan, they used rupees.

We were taking the same security that we did the day before. We followed the same procedure of going to the range and doing a test fire, and by 10:30 A.M. we were on our way to Gayan. It was a very uneventful trip, much different from the day before. We stopped along the way and ate lunch. Brady picked a hilltop that provided a clear observation of the valley; we could see for miles around. Thompson pointed out the route we would be taking on our way back to the firebase. He said we never take the same route back. If we did, we would be very vulnerable to an ambush.

After a fifteen-minute stop, we made our way to Gayan. The village was much different from Wrice. As we entered the village, swarms of kids ran up to us. Thompson tossed out a handful of hard candies; the gunship ahead of us tossed them bottled water and packs from the MREs. As we pulled into the center of the village, the gunships took up a defensive posture. It seemed that every resident of the village came out to see us.

The village elder came up and greeted Thompson, and Thompson introduced him to us. Thompson told him we would be the ones that to deal with now. Warren and I shook hands with him, he invited us to have chi with him, and we accepted. The elder had an entourage of about fifteen people with him, and he motioned to one of them to get the chi. We sat down under a juniper tree and drank the chi. The elder invited some of the members of his entourage to join us. I asked Naime who the members of his entourage were. Naime said they were other ranking members of the village. We told him we were prepared to drill a well, but we had to decide on a location. After some discussion, he agreed to place it in the center of the village.

We finished our chi and walked over to the area where the well would be located. Thompson took a reading with his GPS and marked down the grid coordinates for the location. There must have been three hundred people standing around watching us, and I was beginning to feel uncomfortable. Brady looked over to me and said, "Where the hell is Warren?" Warren had been walking behind me, so I turned around to see, and now he was gone. I looked at Steve and asked him if he saw Warren. Steve said he was talking to someone and must have wandered off. Now Brady was really mad. He called Riddell, who was in one of the gunships, on the radio and said, "We've got a problem, one of the reservists walked off." There was a building off to our right, an old mosque. The elder wanted to convert it to a school. We walked through the crowd and went into the building. There was Warren, looking the building over. One of the members of the elder's entourage was with him; he spoke a little English, enough to convince Warren to take a look at it. Brady pulled Warren to the side and said, "What the fuck are you doing? Do you have any idea where you are?"

"This guy is a teacher, and he was the one who wanted to start a school," Warren replied.

"I don't give a fuck what he wants to do. This is a very dangerous place; the Taliban would love nothing more than to get a hold of you. They will torture you then kill you. We're not playing games here; this is life and death shit. You have put yourself and the rest of us in a serious situation. You need to get your head out of your ass."

Brady told everyone to get back to the vehicles. I stood there and watched as Brady peeled Warren a new ass. Warren and I both outranked Brady; he was a captain, and Warren and I were both majors. Under normal circumstances, you would never talk to a superior officer that way, but these were not normal circumstances. Brady was a Green Beret, a professional soldier; his training and experience far outweighed ours. We were part-time soldiers. If we were going to survive, we had to listen to him and follow his lead.

We drove to the bazaar, which was on the outskirts of the village. It was just like all the other buildings made of earthen walls. We walked in, and it was very dark; there was a very pungent, musty odor. The shopkeeper was a man who appeared to be in his fifties. He had a graying beard and weathered face. Some items were hanging on the wall, some were displayed on a table, and others were piled on the floor. There were no prices on anything, so if we wanted to buy something, we had to ask him the price. Naime told me that Afghans like to barter. I decided I wanted to buy an Afghan hat, so I had Naime do my bartering; he ended up doing it for everyone.

We loaded up and headed out. We stopped at an intersection on the edge of the village. A road turned off and went up a steep hill. At the top of the hill was Bakka Jan's compound. Riddell and Brady got out of their vehicles and marked the location on their GPS. Brady took some pictures of the roads leading up to and away from the compound with his digital camera. When they finished, they got back into the vehicles and headed back to the firebase.

On our way back, Thompson talked to me about what Warren did. I apologized, and explained how he really wants to help the people here, and he is eager to get something going. The problem was, he always sees the good in people and not the bad; he was a teacher in his civilian job. Thompson said, "The problem here is, he won't get a second chance." I knew the incident would give us a black eye. It was going to be harder now to earn their trust.

8

On Our Own

Fridays were holy days for Muslims. Out of respect, we tried to avoid going on missions on Fridays. Our third day in Lwara was a Friday. Even though we were not leaving the firebase, we still had a lot of things to do. My top priority was to secure the bunker from attacks coming from the east. Tim and I filled sandbags and changed the entrance from the back to the side. It took us a couple of hours, but at least now it was well fortified from both the west and east. Mauldin stopped by while we were working; he laughed and said, “They ain't that good a shot to put a rocket inside that little opening.”

“They probably aren't, but it would just be my luck that they would get a lucky shot right in the center,” I replied.

“Go get a couple of the locals and have them do it for ya.”

“I thought about it, but Tim said he needed something to do.”

Tim said, “Bullshit, you just don't trust them.” Tim was right; I didn't trust them to build something that was going to protect us from a rocket attack. I wanted to make sure it was done right. We all laughed, and Mauldin said the reason he came over was to tell me that we had an operational planning meeting at 1:00 P.M. in the Op center.

Warren and I met with Brady, Ross, Thompson, and Stevens. Brady started out by telling us that he had information of a large weapons cache at Bakka Jan's compound. Members of his militia have been moving the weapons from Pakistan to his compound. He also told Brady that Bakka Jan himself has been moving back and forth from Pakistan to Gayan. Brady wanted to put together an operations plan for a raid on his compound. He said it would be a large mission, and just about everyone on the firebase would be involved. He had put in a request for close air support and was waiting to hear back on it.

Brady looked at me and said, "I want your team to be the blocking force at the intersection we were at yesterday. Do you think you can handle it? You can have one of the gunships along with your two vehicles."

I responded with a big, "Hoooah." (Hoooah is Army slang for yes.) Our mission was to be a blocking force at the intersection of the road that went to Bakka Jan's compound and the main road heading out of Gayan. We would have our two vehicles along with a gunship. This was the intersection that we stopped at the day before as we headed out of Gayan. Brady took several pictures and printed them out for us. It was a wide-open intersection, with no cover or concealment. There were some buildings across from the intersection on the main road that led into the village. We were going to set up and block off the intersection, making sure no one went up the road during the raid.

It was about a half mile from the intersection to Bakka Jan's residence. Brady wanted to do the mission as soon as possible; his plan was to do it on Sunday. We worked on the plan for a couple of hours. We couldn't go any farther until we heard back from Bagram to see if we got the close air support. Brady said he would call a meeting as soon as he got word from Bagram. Warren and I went back to our tent, met with our team, and gave them an overview of the mission. I was glad that they had some confidence in us to handle the mission. Thompson, Burke, and Riddell would also be with us, so I'm sure that played a part in Brady giving us the mission. They were Green Berets, and they would know what to do; we would just follow their lead.

Naime came over to our tent that afternoon. I was getting my laundry together to turn in for cleaning. He said, "Mike, my good friend, I would like some blue jeans. How could I get them?"

"You want blue jeans, Naime? Why?"

"I want to look hip. You know, like ones in movies." In Afghanistan, typical male outfits were "one size fits all" pants that were cinched tight with a rope belt and a shirt that hung down to the knees. I liked Naime; he was doing a good job, so I took him over to my tuff box and pulled out a pair of my jeans and gave them to him. I also gave him a tee shirt, a sweatshirt, and a baseball cap. I told him that if he was going to wear the jeans, he had to have the rest of the outfit.

My jeans were big on him; I weighed twenty pounds more than he. "The next time I talk with my wife, I will have her send me a pair of jeans that are the right size for you," I said. He was so excited he couldn't wait to put them on. After that, Naime never wore the traditional clothes again.

Every night, a team would go out on foot patrol. They would be looking for insurgents operating in the area. Many times, the patrols would come across rockets that were aimed at the firebase and hooked up to a timer. If they found a rocket, they would blow it up in place. The patrols usually consisted of four or five members from one of the A-teams. The 82nd also helped out with foot patrols. If one of the patrols ended up in trouble, or if they found something, they would radio back to the person manning the radio in the Op center. The person manning the radio was the lifeline for that patrol. This was our first night on radio duty and, as always, I volunteered to cover it for our team. I wanted to make sure I learned the radio so I could help the rest of my team when they had the duty. My shift lasted from 7:00 to 11:00 P.M. I relieved one of the guys from the 82nd, Corporal Stan Morris. He was a tall redhead from Alabama. When he talked he had a strong southern drawl. He had been in the Army now for three years; he was married and had two kids. He was in the mortar section, one of the ones I had watched the other night during the rocket attack. He was in the chow tent during lunch, and I sat and talked with him. He was going to make a career of the army, just like his father and grandfather before him. Both his father and grandfather served in the 82nd. He told me the story of how his grandfather jumped into Normandy on D-Day with the 82nd. I told him my father served in WWII also. As we were talking, I told him I had radio duty that night, but I was a little concerned because I didn't have any experience with the satellite radio systems. He said, "Don't worry sir, I'll teach ya'll everything ya'll need to know. Ya'll are replacing me on the radio tonight."

"That's great! I'll need all the help I can get."

I reported to the Op center, and Stan was all ready for me. Every unit had a call sign, and ours was Mike 22. Stan made me up a list of the units with their call signs. He told me that tonight, Beast 35 was on patrol, and the call sign for the firebase was Serpent 76. They were operating on the hill west of the firebase. He said they would be calling in a little later for an illumination fire. "They will be giving you their grid location and the location they want the illumination fire. Then you will have to pass that information on to the mortar section."

The mortar section would fire two illumination rounds that would explode in the sky. These rounds would burn very bright, and attached to them was a parachute that allowed the round to fall very slowly to the ground. The rounds would light up a large area and allow the troops on the ground see what was around them. It was used to disrupt insurgents and keep them from placing rockets around the surrounding hilltops. I was really pissed off at the training we got at Ft. Bragg. Communications was a critical part of our mission, and we got very little training on the use of the radios. They showed them to us, but they weren't operational, so I didn't get a chance to practice it. They were much different from the old Viet Nam era PRC-77 radio we used when I was in the infantry. I couldn't have asked for a better trainer, though. Stan sat with me for two hours, showed me how to use the radio and change the batteries if needed, and he wouldn't leave until I had confidence using it. Fortunately, for my first night on the radio, it was quiet. At 10:30, Beast 35 called in the illumination mission. I passed on the coordinates to the mortars, and the illumination went off without a hitch.

I made it back to the tent around 11:30 P.M. Everyone else was already asleep. I hung up my vest, helmet, and rifle on the tent pole behind my cot and put my boots on the floor right next to my cot. I made sure they were all ready to slip on if I needed them. I was real tired; as soon as my head hit the pillow, I was out.

"INCOMING, INCOMING, INCOMING," the guard on the tower yelled, and the air horn went off. I jumped up and spun around on my cot. I got a boost of adrenalin, and my heart was racing. I found my boots and slipped them on, and my vest and helmet were right there on the pole. As I put them on, I heard an explosion. It was south of the firebase at the bottom of the hill. Everyone got out of the tent and made it to the bunkers.

"INCOMING, INCOMING, INCOMING," then a flash and explosion, and the ground shook. That one hit the Hesco on the east side of the firebase. Just then I heard another rocket screaming over the bunker, and it exploded out past the AMF area. I realized we were being fired on from two different directions. I heard the guards at the front of the firebase open up with their 240 machine gun. I strained to see what they were shooting at but couldn't see anything. Tim and Roger were with me in the bunker, and they couldn't see anything, either. The soldier on the FLIR yelled, "I've got movement on the southern hill!" This must have been what the guards on the front gate were firing at. The mortar team sprang to action. They began to turn the guns to the south; the soldier on the FLIR began yelling out the coordinates.

Then the soldier in the rear tower yelled, "INCOMING, INCOMING, INCOMING." A rocket was fired from the east. The mortar team ran back to their bunker as the rocket screamed overhead and landed in the LZ. Now I could hear the .50 caliber from one of the gunships engaging a target to the south. The mortar section ran back to the tubes. I could hear the mortar sergeant give the directions, then WHUMP, WHUMP, a few seconds later I could hear the concussion of the rounds slam the hill to the south.

"Fire for effect!" the soldier on the FLIR screamed. The mortars fired a volley of ten rounds. The rounds pounded the hillside with one explosion after another that echoed through the valley, sounding like a violent thunderstorm.

"INCOMING, INCOMING, INCOMING," screamed the guard in the tower. There was a bright flash then a tremendous explosion, and the sandbags shifted. Tim, Roger, and I were knocked to the ground. It felt like the air was being sucked out of my lungs. The rocket slammed into the Hesco Barrier right next to the bunker. The mortar team swung the tubes back to the east. They got the coordinates from the FLIR, again the mortar sergeant gave them the direction, and, WHUMP, WHUMP, the rounds slammed the mountain to the east.

"Adjust fire, five degrees north, three degrees east."

"Roger, grid five degree north, three degrees east."

WHUMP, WHUMP, a couple seconds of silence, then two explosions. "That's it, fire for effect!"

"Roger, fire for effect!" With that, another ten rounds were fired on the eastern hill. The explosions reverberated through the valley. The machine guns went quiet; a blue haze from the mortar and machine gunfire filtered through the firebase. The FLIR scanned the two hills, and there was no movement on either one. After about five minutes, the "all clear" sign was given. I went over and checked with Warren, Steve, and Fred; everyone was okay. Two rockets hit the Hesco barriers, and both were fired from the eastern hill. Fortunately, no one was injured.

I went over to the Op center. Brady was sending in a SITREP (Situation Report) to Bagram on the attack. He was requesting an emergency resupply for the morning. This was the fourth attack on the firebase in the last seven days. The mortar section was getting critically low on rounds. The mortars were the primary defensive weapons of the firebase. Bagram approved the emergency resupply and scheduled it for 10:00 A.M. Brady told me that he needed our team to assist with the resupply. We would help unload the helicopter and take the ammo up to the firebase.

I walked out of the tent and over by the bunker to survey the damage done by the rocket attack that night. One rocket landed about two feet from the bunker I was in; there was shrapnel all over. As I was looking around, Thompson came over. He said, "You're not going to believe this. We got the word from Bagram; we're ex-filling on the resupply bird."

"You're kidding me."

"No, our command wants us out of here."

"What about our mission tomorrow?"

"Don't worry, you guys are doing good. I talked to Brady, and he thinks you can handle it." I couldn't believe it: our training consisted of three days. It would be up to me to lead our team on the Gayan mission.

The helicopters touched down at 10:00 A.M. We unloaded the ammo, shook hands with Thompson, Burke, and Riddell, and watched them board the helicopter. As the helicopter took off, the reality sunk in. We were now on our own. We didn't get the training we needed at Fort Bragg, and we didn't get the two weeks of "left seat, right seat" here. I knew if we were going to survive, we needed to rely on our civilian experiences and our instincts.

Brady called a meeting at the Op center; the raid on Bakka Jan's compound was a go. Two F-16s will be providing fire support on the movement to Gayan during the raid and on the movement back to the firebase. "Now that Thompson's team is gone, you CA guys are on your own. I still need your team to be the blocking force at the intersection."

"We can handle it," I replied. The mission was actually a civil affairs mission, dealing with civilians on the battlefield. Whenever Americans showed up in the village, everyone would come out to see what was going on. The last time we were in Gayan, we drew a large crowd. Our mission was to keep the residents safe and away from the raid by making sure no one went up the road to the compound. We would also be the forward security element, engaging any hostile forces that might try a counterattack. Brady asked if we were up to speed on the .50 caliber. We should have received some familiarization training on the .50 caliber and the Mark 19 at Fort Bragg, but we didn't get it—another missed training opportunity. I told him some members of our team hadn't fired one in quite some time. He said he would have Mauldin take us to the range and get everyone up to speed.

That afternoon, I held a briefing with our team and discussed the mission with them. I could tell everyone was a little apprehensive. We had just been through four rocket attacks where we had the security of the firebase. Now we were going on a mission away from the firebase where there was a very real possibility of direct combat. This was going to be a big test, and I was a little apprehensive, too. Steve was going to be the team sergeant for this mission. He would make sure all of our equipment was ready and that everyone on the team had everything needed for the mission.

The next morning, we left for Gayan at 8:00 A.M. The mission consisted of both Special Forces teams, the SOT-A team, our CA team, three squads from the 82nd, and six AMF—a total of seventy-five soldiers and twelve vehicles. There was a fifteen-man security element left back at the firebase. As we made our way to Gayan, the F-16s circled above. It was a reassuring feeling having them with us. Everyone knew what their role was; having the pictures ahead of time, we knew where to place the vehicles. On the convoy to Gayan, we were the last three vehicles in line. When we hit the intersection, the first nine vehicles turned left and went up the hill to the compound. My vehicle was next, and we took up a position on the west side of the intersection. I placed the gunship in the center of the intersection, and our other vehicle took up a position on the east side. We dismounted the vehicles and took cover behind them. Tim stayed in the turret of the gunship and manned the .50 caliber.

It wasn't long before a crowd started to gather across the road. I had Naime tell them they needed to stay back. We were in place for about ten minutes when there was an explosion coming from the compound. The breach team was using C-4 explosives to enter. The crowd was now becoming agitated, and there were people gathering on the rooftop of one of the buildings. The F-16s went screaming overhead as a show of force. The problem with that was that it drew a bigger crowd; there must have been four hundred people across from us. Both buildings now had people on the roofs. I spotted a group of five males by the corner of one of the buildings, and they were huddled up talking. One kept looking around. As I looked through the binoculars, I could see that three of them were armed with AK-47s. This in itself was not unusual, because everyone in Afghanistan was allowed to own one AK-47, and many people carried them openly. But their physical actions concerned me. I was concerned that they were planning an attack on us or trying to figure out how to get up to the compound. Steve was on the other side of the intersection. I called to him to get a look. He didn't like what he saw, either. I called out to the team, and I had Tim orient the .50 caliber toward them.

The crowd continued to grow, and as it grew, they became more vocal. I had been around large, angry crowds before; it doesn't take much for them to turn on you. I asked Naime what he thought. He didn't like the situation either; he could hear some yelling at us to leave. As I watched the three armed individuals, I caught a flash from the rooftop—someone was using a mirror as a signal. They were communicating something to someone; my mind raced with all the possibilities, none of which was good. The armed men had moved about fifty yards down the road from us, and it appeared they were about to cross the road. My concern was if they crossed the road, they could head up the hill to the compound or try to attack us from behind. Their group had grown; there must have been ten to fifteen of them now. I knew we had to do something. If we let the situation continue, we could lose control of the crowd.

I remembered back to my days in law enforcement when I was on the Addison Police Department. It was Halloween night, and a large crowd of about fifty people had formed outside of one of the bars on Main Street. They had all been drinking, and I knew if the crowd was to continue their unruly behavior, a riot could break out. Cars and storefronts would be damaged, and people would be injured. I called for backup; once they arrived, we told the crowd to disperse, and they refused. I ended up using a tear gas canister to break up the crowd. The tear gas worked, and the crowd dispersed with no damage or injuries.

I knew our team had to take some action here just like I had done. I directed Tim to aim the .50 caliber down the road in front of the group preparing to cross the road and to fire some warning shots. Tim opened up with the .50 caliber; he fired five rounds down the road. The group stopped and hit the ground. When Tim stopped firing, they got up and ran off in the opposite direction. I then told Tim to fire some rounds over the heads of the people on the roof where they were signaling with the mirror. He fired another five-round burst over their heads. The crowd started running back toward town. I called Brady on the radio and advised him we had fired some warning shots to disperse a large crowd that had formed. Brady told me they would be done in about fifteen minutes. The main crowd had dispersed; firing the warning shots worked. Tim said, "Good call; that was awesome!"

"We had to do something; I figured the .50 caliber would get their attention."

"You should've seen them on this side; they couldn't run fast enough. They kept tripping over each other as they were running away," Steve said. I made the right decision. I knew if I let it go on, we could have had some serious problems. A few minutes later, the convoy made its way down the hill. We took up the same positions we had on the way back to the firebase. I was glad it was over; I was able to relax a little on the way back.

We met in the Op center for the AAR. Brady started out telling us the mission was a success. They found a small weapons cache hidden in the compound. They recovered twenty AK-47s, ten 107-mm rockets, and five cases of 60-mm mortar rounds. Bakka Jan was not at the compound, but there had been recent activity there. Brady reviewed how the mission went from start to finish and what each unit participating in the raid did. When he got to the CA team he said, "A big kudos to the CA team, you guys did an outstanding job! How big did the crowd get down there?"

"We had close to four hundred people," I responded.

"I knew you were going to get a big crowd. Every time we go to Gayan, large crowds come out to look at us. I bet that .50 cal got their attention."

"It was the best crowd dispenser I have ever used." Everyone in the Op center laughed.

"When I send my SITREP into Bagram tonight, I'm going to let them know what a great job you did. I don't think Thompson and his team couldn't have done any better." I knew then we had taken a big step in securing their respect. It also gave us confidence in ourselves.

9

The Jurga

We were settling into the day-to-day operations at the firebase. We were lacking some important pieces of equipment, the most important one being a shower bag. The firebase had one shower stall. It was a small building constructed of plywood, about four feet by four feet, with a slanted roof. There was a wood floor with holes drilled in it for the water to drain and a hook in the ceiling to hang a shower bag. Nobody ever told us we needed a shower bag. None of us had ever deployed before, with the exception of Roger. He deployed to Saudi Arabia during the Persian Gulf War, but his time was spent in a barracks in Riyadh, so he had no idea we needed one. With the temperature hovering around one hundred degrees, we were dirty and sweaty and needed a shower.

Tim went scrounging around the firebase to see if he could find one. Tim was great at bartering; everyone on the firebase knew he had all those movies, so he struck a deal with the 82nd. They would let us use one of their shower bags, and they could pick out a movie each night to watch. It was an old Army-issue canvas shower bag. The civilian camp showers were far superior to the Army-issue shower bags. We found out everyone brought their own camp shower, which was why they were so quick to give up the Army one.

We had an Army water buffalo (water storage tank on wheels) that was filled each week at a local spring. The firebase had purchased an Afghan water heater to heat the water for a shower. The water heater consisted of a three-gallon water tank and spigot mounted on top of a steel fire chamber. A person who needed hot water would fill the water chamber, then build a fire in the fire chamber. It was very time consuming to get hot water, so most of the time we filled up our ten-gallon water containers and sat them in the sun to warm up.

The firebase had a large generator that provided electricity to every tent. We didn't know we would have this; if we had, we would have brought some other things with us. Being reservists definitely had its drawbacks when it came to combat preparedness, as well as respect among active soldiers, but one of the good things was our civilian connections. I decided to make a list of things that our team could use that would make our deployment more bearable. I called Lorrie and gave her our list. The most important item was the camp showers. I asked her to see if she could get six of them, one for each of us. I also asked her to send us a coffee pot, Dunkin Donuts® coffee, a television, a DVD player, flashlights, headlamps, food, and anything homemade. She said she would go and get what we needed and send them out. It took about two weeks from the time she mailed something to reach me at the firebase. She had a hard time finding six camp showers. The local Dick's Sporting Goods had to special order the showers from other stores. She was able to get everything on my list and mailed it out a couple of days later.

We had a meeting in the Op center to discuss the recent attacks on the firebase. Ross wanted to hold a Jurga (meeting of all the local village elders) to discuss the attacks on the base. He said it would be a good opportunity for us to plan some humanitarian missions with the elders and gain their support. He wanted to hold the meeting at the foot of the firebase. Warren and I thought this would be a great opportunity to meet all the elders and find out what we could do for them. Ross said that most of them were former members of the Taliban but, in typical Afghan style, they loved to barter, and we were in position to offer them much more than the Taliban could. Brady came up with an idea to pay a reward to anyone for giving us the location of a weapons cache. If we successfully retrieved the cache, we would then pay that person. If it was a large cache, we would pay them $100, which was several thousand in rupees. If it was a small cache, we would pay between $25 and $50. All of us liked that idea. Brady told me to make that offer to the elders at the Jurga. Ross said he would put the word out that we would hold the Jurga in three days.

Warren and I walked back to our tent and met Steve outside. We sat down next to the bunker and talked about some of the humanitarian projects we could start. Warren wanted to get a school going as soon as possible. He wanted to go back and talk to Dr. Nikeeb. I wasn't keen on starting one there, and I told him about our concerns with Dr. Nikeeb. I was all for starting one, but I didn't want it to be associated with him. We also talked about doing a Med Cap (bringing in doctors and veterinarians to treat the locals) and giving away blankets and clothing that had been sent to us from different organizations back home. We had been sitting there talking and planning for about a half an hour when there was a loud explosion to our east. There were three compounds about 2500 yards east of the firebase. The explosion came from this vicinity. We grabbed our gear, and everyone took up fighting positions. We waited for a few minutes then got the word that someone was at the front gate who needed an interpreter. I went over to the interpreters' bunker and told Naime to come with me. We walked out to the gate. Brady and Ross were already there. There was a man there who appeared to be in his mid thirties. He had a lot of blood on him, and he was very upset. Naime asked him what was wrong. They talked for a minute, and Naime looked to me and said, "This man's son has been injured. He found something by their compound and was playing with it when it exploded. He said he is badly injured." Brady called Spycher on the radio and told him he needed the QRF to check on a possible injury. Brady was going to have his medic, Sam Arnold, go with them. I told Brady that Naime and I would also go.

Ross said, "This looks legit, but be careful, you never know." I hopped in the first gunship with the man.

The man looked over to me and said in English, "Please help him." I was really surprised he spoke English.

"We will do everything we can," I said. It was about a three-minute ride. We pulled up, and the QRF went into an immediate defensive position. We could see a group of people standing around a boy lying on the ground. Arnold, Naime, and I ran up to him, and Doc Arnold knelt beside him. Both of his legs and arms were severely wounded, and he had shrapnel wounds all over his upper body. Doc applied a tourniquet to his left leg and arm. During one of the rocket attacks, a rocket landed short of the firebase and didn't detonate. The boy found it a few days later and began playing with it, and it detonated. Doc radioed back to the firebase requesting a medivac (medical evacuation by helicopter). Doc stabilized him as best as he could, and we loaded him in one of the gunships and transported him back to the firebase.

Doc said he was really lucky to be alive. I asked the father what his name was, and he replied, "Mir Shir Khan."

It was a thirty-minute flight from Bagram for the medivac. Mir Shir Khan's English was not nearly as good as Naime's so I had Naime tell him that we would be flying him to a military hospital in Bagram where they would take care of him. Mir Shir Khan had two other sons whom he couldn't leave, so he would be unable to go with him. I told Naime to reassure him that he would be in good hands. I also had Naime tell him that I would contact Bagram, and they would give me a daily update on his condition, and he could come to the firebase every day to find out how he was doing. We loaded the boy on the medivac and sent him to Bagram. I went to the Op center, sent a SITREP advising Bagram of the situation, and requested them to track the boy's progress.

Mir Shir Khan was at the front gate waiting for Naime and me. He was pleased I had an update on his son. Bagram communicated that the boy was in serious but stable condition. He awaited transfer to another hospital, as he already lost his left leg and was facing the prospect of losing the other.

Mir Shir Khan was grateful for our help and promise that we would attempt a visit between him and his son. We continued talking and learned what had brought him to Afghanistan. He said he was from Pakistan but encountered problems with his tribe. He moved his three sons to Afghanistan. His conflict continued in the Lwara Valley, because the residents belonged to the Pepoli tribe and considered Mir Shir Khan an outcast. His native tribe in Pakistan did not want him. He went on to explain his difficult living circumstances and desire to work, but no one in Lwara would associate with him.

"What is it you do?" I asked.

"I'm a teacher."

I grinned as Warren entered the tent just as Mir Shir Khan made this announcement. I looked to Warren and said, "We just found our teacher."

Warren followed my pointing finger to Mir Shir Khan. I introduced him as the father of the injured boy. Warren walked over to the teacher and shook his hand. Warren said, "I'm sorry about your son, but he's in very good hands. Where did you teach?"

"Seven years in Karachi."

Warren nodded. This was a definite direction for him to start the school project. Warren shared his plan.

"We want to start a school here in the valley. Are you interested in being the teacher?"

Mir Shir Khan gave an enthusiastic nod. Warren and I smiled. Warren invited him to the Jurga to discuss the school plan, and he accepted. He thanked us for our kindness, most likely the first he experienced since moving to the Lwara Valley. Even as an outcast, I wondered if he had any information about the locals. I asked, "Do you know Dr. Nikeeb? He also wants to start a school."

Mir Shir Khan's smile disappeared. He replied, "I know him. He is Pakistani. I don't like him."

Warren's eyebrows rose. Warren asked, "What don't you like about him?"

"He isn't what he says he is."

I jumped in the conversation by asking, "You mean he isn't a doctor?" Mir Shir Khan gave an emphatic no gesture.

"He is no doctor. He only wants to hurt people."

I thanked Mir Shir Khan for the information, and I told him not to tell any of the other locals that we talked. He said he wouldn't—no one would talk to him anyway. I walked Mir Shir Khan to the front gate, then I went over to the Op center. Brady was in there, and I told him about the conversation I just had with Mir Shir Khan.

"I was talking with the father of the boy who was injured yesterday. He knows Dr. Nikeeb, and he says he is not a doctor," I said to Brady.

"That's good; I'm hearing the same thing. Nikeeb is going to be at the Jurga tomorrow, and we need to keep our eyes on him."

"I've invited the father of the injured boy. He says he was a teacher in Pakistan, and if we get the school going, he might be our teacher."

"That was lucky. I wasn't sure how you were going to find a teacher. Of course, you can't believe everything these people tell you. He might be looking to get information from you."

"I know you don't know whom you can trust."

The morning of the Jurga, Brady, and Ross sent out security details on all the surrounding hilltops. We were also going to have an inner security detail. Warren and I would be running the Jurga with the elders while the rest of our team would be assisting with the inner security. Ross and Brady didn't want to sit in on the Jurga. They wanted to sit on the side and listen. We had Steve take pictures; many of the elders still had close ties to the Taliban, so Brady and Ross wanted to document who was whom. The SOT-A team had its own interpreter, Muhammad Guhl, nicknamed Johnny. He grew up in Afghanistan then moved to the United States during the Russian invasion. He became an American citizen and went to work for the Department of Defense as an interpreter. None of the other interpreters knew he was originally from Afghanistan and that he spoke Pashtu. Johnny wore an Army uniform and lived in the SOT-A's tent. The interpreters thought he was just one of the soldiers. During the Jurga, he was going to sit and listen to Naime interpret. We wanted to make sure Naime was being honest with us and telling the elders what we wanted him to tell them, and that he was telling us exactly what they were saying. I would continue this practice of testing Naime throughout our stay in Lwara.

At 10:00 A.M., the vehicles carrying the elders began to arrive. It was a sight to see. A little four-door Toyota pickup truck designed to carry five passengers would be loaded with twenty-five people, seven in the cab and eighteen riding in the back. This is how it was for every vehicle that arrived. By the time everyone arrived, there were close to three hundred people. There were twenty elders representing all the villages in the Lwara valley. The AMF brought mats down for us to sit on; they also had their cook make us bread and chi. Warren and I welcomed each elder and thanked him for coming. We sat in a big circle and started the Jurga by serving the bread and chi. Warren thanked everyone for coming, and this Jurga was a beginning of what we hoped to be a long friendship with the Afghan people. He explained that the reason we were here was to find the terrorists who attacked the United States and to help the Afghan people rebuild their country. He wanted them to understand that we were not here to occupy their country like the Russians did. The elders sat there and listened intently; they wanted to hear what we could do for them. I told them we were prepared to drill a well in each village, and we wanted to bring in our doctors to treat their sick and veterinarians to treat their animals. I also said we wanted to start a school in the Lwara valley. One of the elders asked how soon we could do theses things. I told him we would be visiting all of their villages in the next couple of weeks to decide on a well location, and we could bring the doctors out within the next month. They all seemed very happy with that. Warren said we wanted to start a school now. There had never been a school in the valley. One of President Karzai's top priorities was to build schools and provide an education for all Afghan children. During the Taliban reign, only boys were allowed to attend schools; girls were forbidden to attend. The elders talked amongst themselves, and they asked where it would be located. Warren said we would locate it where we were sitting then. One of the elders interrupted and said, "Girls shall not attend school."

"These are different times; the ways of the Taliban are gone, and girls need an education just as much as boys do," I replied.

"Girls cannot be in school with boys!!" The elder was becoming very agitated.

"If we ran the school for boys in the morning then had the girls come in the afternoon, that way they would be separated, and the girls could still get an education," Warren suggested. The elders talked amongst themselves again. I leaned over to Naime and asked him what they were saying. Naime said that most of them didn't care if we ran the school, but a couple of them were against girls attending. Some of them were concerned that if they didn't agree, we wouldn't help out their villages. The elders continued to talk for a couple of minutes, and then one said, "We agree on the school, but the boys and girls must be separated."

"That's great; we will run separate times for them."

I then said to the group, "There is one more thing we need to talk about, and that is the attacks we have been having on our base. We need your help to stop these attacks. We know there are weapons moving across the border from Pakistan, and these weapons are being used against us. If you or any members of your villages tell us where these weapons are and we find these weapons, we will pay whoever gave us the information."

"How much will you pay us?"

"If there are a lot of weapons, 2,000 rupees; less weapons 500 to 1,000 rupees. It all depends how many there are."

The elders didn't say anything, but several of them turned and looked at each other. I knew we struck a chord with them. Time would tell how successful it would be. We finished the Jurga by thanking them for coming, and we told them we would like to have another Jurga next month; they all agreed to meet again next month.

After the Jurga, we met back in the Op center to go over the meeting. Brady told us we did a nice job with the elders. Now we had to get out to the villages and show them we were serious with the promises we made them. Brady said, "They're running the show here in the valley. They know who is running the weapons and who is shooting at us. We need to win their support if we are going to have any success."

"I'm going to put in a request to Bagram to send us the humanitarian meals and blankets they have stored. If we can get them on our next resupply, we can start visiting the villages and hand out the meals and blankets. That would be an immediate response to show we are serious," I responded.

"That's a great idea. The faster we move, the quicker they will be in giving us information."

"Johnny, how did Naime do?"

"He did very well; his translation was right on the money. You got a good interpreter." That was what I wanted to hear. Naime was fitting right in with our team; this information helped to strengthen our confidence in him. I would never fully trust him, nor would we ever talk about missions with him. We never told him where we were going or when we would be back. He would just report to our tent in the morning, then get in the vehicle and go with us.

"We would like to get the school going as soon as possible. We are going to need some sort of shelter. Any ideas?" Warren asked.

"We have an extra tent you guys can have," Ross replied.

"Perfect. Once we get the school going, we will build a permanent building."

Warren and I went back to the tent and had a team meeting. Steve had taken several pictures of all the attendees at the Jurga and he was in the process of printing them out. Brady and Ross wanted copies so they could identify who was whom. I wanted a copy so when we went to a village, we would know who the elder was. I asked everyone how the security detail went. They said there were no problems. I said I thought the Jurga was a success. Warren told everyone we were going to start the school very soon. "Ross is going to let us use one of their spare tents until we can get a permanent building constructed. Mike has found a teacher, the father of the boy that was injured," Warren informed the team.

"I will meet with Mir Shir Khan and go over with him our expectations for the school. I will also put in a request to Bagram for school supplies. I remember seeing cases of school supplies when we were there," I said.

"We are also going to visit all the villages and hand out humanitarian blankets and meals. Hopefully, we can get everything on our next resupply."

It was a good feeling knowing that we were actually going to provide some humanitarian relief to the residents of the Lwara Valley. I could tell that everyone on the team was excited about our future and doing our civil affairs mission.

10

The Capture

The resupply was scheduled for 1:00 P.M. Bagram sent a message that we were getting everything we requested. We had a couple of hours before the resupply, so Tim and I dug out the tent we were going to use for the school. As we were inventorying all the pieces, I got word that Mir Shir Khan was at the front gate requesting to see me. I brought him in and took him over to where we were working on the tent. I told him the Jurga had approved the school, and we would like him to be the teacher; we would pay him 500 rupees per week ($25.00 U.S. dollars). He grinned from ear to ear. He said, "You are so kind, thank you so much."

"I got word from Bagram your son is in stable condition and doing well. I am working on arrangements for you to fly to Bagram and visit him."

"You don't know how happy you made me."

I didn't tell Mir Shir Khan that his son lost his left leg, and they weren't sure if they could save his right leg. His son was very lucky that the rocket didn't fully detonate. It was the propulsion part of the rocket that exploded. Had the rocket fully detonated, he would have been killed instantly. I told him that we would like to start the school in a couple of days. We were going to set up a tent as a temporary school then build a permanent building later. Warren and I would sit down with him and discuss the curriculum he would be teaching. Mir Shir Khan was very grateful for his new opportunity and for the care his son was getting.

We had the security teams deployed around the hilltops as we waited for the helicopters. Spycher reminded us to make sure we took our goggles with us and to get something to wrap around our noses and mouths. When the helicopters land, they would kick up a lot of dust, and it would be hard to see and breathe. About five minutes later, we could hear the distinct roar of the helicopter rotor blades as they echoed through the valley. In a typical resupply, we would get one or maybe two Chinook helicopters. As we watched the helicopters crest the mountaintop, we began counting—one, two, three, four Chinooks and two Apache gunships. "Holy shit, what the hell are they bringing us!" asked one of the soldiers. As the Chinooks landed, they kicked up a tremendous dust cloud. Spycher was right. We drove up and began loading our vehicles as the crew chiefs were throwing the supplies out the back. All four Chinooks were filled to capacity; it was obvious this was going to take several trips back and forth before we got everything up to the firebase. It took nearly twenty minutes to get everything up to the firebase. In a typical resupply, it's a five-minute job.

We sorted through everything and stacked all the humanitarian supplies (consisting of blankets, meals, and clothing) and the school supplies (consisting of paper, pencils, rulers, chalk, and book bags) in one of the empty supply tents that belonged to the 82nd. We took all of our personal packages back to our tent. It was like Christmas as we ripped open our packages to see what we got. My wife Lorrie came through—she sent me six camp showers. I gave everyone on the team one. She also sent me the television, DVD player, and coffee pot with coffee creamer and sugar. I couldn't wait to take a shower and have a good cup of coffee. We also got homemade cookies and brownies. It sure was nice to eat something other than MREs or T-Rats. Brady came by our tent and said, "I can't believe how much shit you guys got! The 96th never got stuff like this."

"That's the difference between active and reserve Civil Affairs; we have the connections and they don't."

Brady laughed, "I guess so. Hopefully, getting that stuff out to the villages will show the elders we mean what we say, and they will start turning over some caches to us."

"I know, I want to start delivering the blankets and food to the villages as soon as possible," Warren said.

Brady was looking at the boxes our families sent us. "I don't believe it, you got a television and DVD player sent to ya!"

"Sure did, plus a coffee pot and camp showers! Look what Steve got, fifteen new movies and all those cookies and brownies." Steve gave Brady a couple cookies and a brownie.

"These are great! I haven't had anything homemade in quite awhile. I need to come by here more often." We all laughed. It was nice getting things from home. Lorrie also sent me a couple local newspapers and a video she and the boys made. We sat around for the next couple of hours, reading the newspapers and eating all the cookies and brownies. Word spread fast throughout the firebase that we got a lot of goodies, and everyone came by to see what we got and sample some of our food. We were the only ones on the firebase who got packages. Everyone else, if they were lucky, just got a letter from home. I felt sorry for the guys who didn't get anything; living in these extremely harsh conditions, the only thing they have to look forward to is mail from home. I didn't mind sharing what I got; as a matter of fact, I enjoyed it, and everyone who came to our tent was really appreciative. It really helped us bond with the other members of the firebase.

The excitement of the resupply from the day before was now over, and it was time to get back to work. Tim, Fred, and Roger took the tent down to the foot of the hill where we held the Jurga and set it up. While they were doing this, Warren, Naime, and I met with Mir Shir Khan to discuss the curriculum he would be teaching. I asked him what the ages of his students were and what did he teach. Mir Shir Khan said that his students were boys between the age of six and sixteen. His class size varied from fifteen to thirty, depending on the time of year. He taught the *Koran,* math, Pashtu, reading, writing, and history. Warren and I thought that would be a good start. We didn't have any idea how many kids would show up or what their ages would be. Since most of the kids in the valley had never had any type of formal education, we were sure they would all be at the same level. We didn't have any Pashtu books, so Mir Shir Khan was going to have to create everything himself. He said that wouldn't be a problem because, in his last school, he didn't have any books, either. He could do everything on the chalkboard. Luckily for us, there was chalkboard paint in the school supplies, and there was plenty of plywood on the base, so we could build a chalkboard for him.

We walked over to the supply tent and went through the school supplies; we had enough supplies for thirty students. Mir Shir Khan put the book bags together with pencils, paper, rulers, and chalk in each. Warren and I got a piece of plywood and some two-by-four lumber and built the chalkboard. When we were in Ft. Bragg, we bought a rechargeable battery operated tool kit with a drill and two saws. At the time, I wasn't sure we would ever use it or how we were going to recharge the batteries. Now I was really glad we bought it. I could see we would be using it a lot. When we finished, we loaded all the school supplies and the chalkboard on our vehicle and drove it down to the school tent.

Where we located the school tent, the guards at the front gate acted as an overwatch position for us, providing us with security when we were there. While we were setting the school up, we had several local kids stop by and ask what was going on. Mir Shir Khan told them this was going to be their new school. They all seemed very excited and wanted to know when it would start. Mir Shir Khan told them, "Saturday, three days from now." We finished getting everything set up and headed back up to the firebase. We had a meeting in the Op center to discuss our upcoming missions to visit the villages and distribute our HA (Humanitarian Assistance) supplies. Mir Shir Khan stayed at the school, tinkering around and getting everything ready for the opening; he was like a kid in a toy store.

There were ten villages in our AO. Wrice was the farthest north, Gayan in the south, Shawjal Khel in the west, then spread around between these were Maritz, Sendi Khwlah, Arghamel, Shadohany, Kaber Khel, Dawerary, and Merbeck. With the exception of Gayan, most of these villages ranged in population from 150 to 300 residents. Warren and I met Brady and Ross in the Op center. They were putting together an OPCON for the next two days. Ross wanted to visit the villages to the northwest of the firebase (Shawjal Khel, Maritz, Sendi Khwlah, and Arghamel) first, then the villages of Shadohany, Kaber Khel, Dawerary, and Merbeck the next day.

The village of Merbeck was a reported hotbed of Taliban activity. Brady wanted to recon the village for future reference. The only villages that Brady's or Ross's teams had visited before we arrived were Gayan and Arghamel. They were looking forward to visiting the other villages and gathering intelligence on them. Our part of the mission was to perform an assessment of the village and distribute some of the humanitarian aid. The assessment would include designating protected targets, medical and humanitarian needs, and availability of clean drinking water. Protected targets consisted of hospitals, mosques, schools, and cemeteries. We would determine where in the village any of these places were located and plot their grid location. We would report their locations to Bagram, and they would be placed on a protected target list. During combat operations, those locations were not allowed to become targets of direct or indirect fire. We finished the meeting and headed back to our tent to brief our team on the upcoming missions.

We spent the next day visiting the first four villages. The elders were very happy to see us. We gave each elder five cases of humanitarian meals and two hundred blankets. None of the villages had working wells, so we proposed a well for each village. Each village had a mosque and cemetery but no schools or hospitals. The elders were all very grateful for the food, blankets, and proposed water well. We reinforced with them that we were here to help them, not fight them.

Our last stop was the village of Arghamel. It was located about five miles from the firebase. We visited a bazaar located in Arghamel. The bazaar was located in a small building in the center of town. It was dark and had a strong, pungent, musty odor. There were a shopkeeper and his son running it. He was very happy to see us, and he shook our hand and invited us to look around. There was no organization to the store. Clothes were mixed in with the food and hand tools. Some things were displayed on the floor and some on small tables. There was goat meat hanging from a hook; it was one hundred degrees outside, and the meat was covered with flies. A local Afghan came in while we were looking around and bought some of the meat. The shopkeeper took the meat down, swatted the flies off, cut a piece off, and sold it to him. When he finished with the transaction, he hung the remaining piece back on the hook. I couldn't imagine eating it. Naime did the bartering for us. I found three children's vests that I bought for my sons, along with three Afghan hats. I also bought myself a scarf that I could wrap around my face during the sandstorms, and an Afghan hat. Everyone ended up buying some kind of souvenir. The shopkeeper thanked us for coming and invited us back anytime.

We visited the last four villages the next day. We got the same reception from the elders in Dawerary, Kaber Khel, and Shadohany as we had the day before. People came out and greeted us, elders invited us for chi, and everyone was happy. Merbeck, though, was a different story. We were greeted by the elder, and he told us he didn't want us in his village and he didn't want anything from us. The village was eerily quiet. Brady and Ross moved their teams and gunships to the top of the hill next to the village so they could provide an overwatch. Tim was taking some pictures for us when the elder spotted him and began yelling at him to stop taking pictures. Spycher's team had dismounted their vehicles when we entered the village, and when the elder began yelling, they moved closer to us. Brady had a camera with him, and I knew he was taking pictures, too. I looked over to Ross, and he gave the signal for us to leave, so we got back into our vehicles and headed out. On our way out of the village, Brady called on the radio and had us look at the building on the southwest side at our nine o'clock. There was an antenna on it, a sure sign of Taliban activity.

When we returned to the firebase, we had our after-action review in the Op center.

"Another good day—we learned a lot, especially about Merbeck," I said.

"Yeah, I told you that I heard Merbeck was full of Taliban supporters. Our visit confirmed that," Brady replied.

"The elder definitely didn't want Tim taking any pictures."

"I know they were hiding something in that building. I got some good pictures, though."

"We need to start working on a CONOP for a Cordon Search there," Ross said.

"We'll see if SOT-A can intercept some chatter coming out of Merbeck. They must be communicating with somebody, with the size of that antenna they have," Brady added. It had been a good two days. We had a good feel for the AO now, and we were doing some positive things for the residents of the valley. We designated eight mosques and seven cemeteries as protected targets. We proposed eight wells and distributed six hundred blankets and four hundred humanitarian meals in the two days. Hopefully, by showing the elders we mean what we say, they would be willing to help us root out the Taliban and Al-Qaeda forces operating in the valley.

It was about 10:00 P.M., and I decided to go over to the Op center and send our SITREP to Bagram and check on Tim, as it was his first night on the radio. Warren usually sent the SITREP, but I needed some practice, so I volunteered to do it. It took me a few minutes to write it up and send it, but it went through without any problem. I sat there and talked to Tim for a while, it was quiet on the radio; the patrol had just returned to the base, and everything was nice and quiet. Tim's shift was almost ready to end, so I decided it was time to head back to the tent and go to bed. The school was opening tomorrow, and I knew Mir Shir Khan would be at the firebase early in the morning.

I just stood up, and a large explosion rocked the Op center. I immediately hit the ground. I heard the air horn, then another explosion.

The firebase was under attack again. Brady came running in the Op center just as the third explosion hit the outside wall. He said they were firing on us from the mountain east of the firebase. The soldier on the FLIR radioed he had a fix on the position, and he had four individuals on the side of the mountain running downhill. Just then I could hear the mortars return fire. Then there was the distant rumbling of the mortar rounds impacting on the mountain. The FLIR radioed that he was still tracking the four individuals, and they were headed for Dr. Nikeeb's compound. Brady radioed Spycher and told him to send the QRF to Dr. Nikeeb's and intercept the four individuals coming off the mountain.

Within three minutes, the QRF was out the front gate and headed to Dr. Nikeeb's compound. I ran back to the tent, grabbed my gear, and checked on the rest of the team. Everyone made it to the bunkers unharmed. The mortar section was in place, waiting for a fire mission if needed. I decided to head back to the Op center and help Tim. Just as I got to the Op center, I heard the QRF firing the .50 caliber, then an all out firefight broke out. The battle raged for about five minutes. The QRF radioed back to the base that they had been engaged by an undetermined number of forces at Dr. Nikeeb's compound. Finally, the shooting stopped. A few minutes later, the QRF radioed that they had three enemy KIA (killed in action), and they had taken two enemy prisoners. The rest of the enemy force had withdrawn.

Spycher returned with the QRF and the two enemy prisoners. He brought them into the Op center; one of the prisoners was Dr. Nikeeb. Spycher said that, when they arrived at the compound, Dr. Nikeeb and about ten others were unloading several 107-mm rockets from a vehicle. The QRF surprised them, and they opened fire on Spycher and the QRF. They returned fire, killing two. The remainder of the enemy force withdrew back up the mountain, but Dr. Nikeeb and his worker could not get away. Ross radioed Bagram and requested they send a helicopter and pick up the two PUCs. Enemy prisoners were now called PUCs, for "person under contact." We did not refer to them as prisoners of war.

Brady said, "I knew he was dirty!"

Nikeeb and his worker sat in the corner of the Op center, their hands shackled and heads down. The next day, a helicopter came and picked up Nikeeb and his worker. It was determined that Nikeeb was not a doctor but a member of Al-Qaeda and had been instrumental in the recent attacks on the firebase.

11

V & T

Warren, Tim, and I were shocked to find twenty-five boys waiting for the school to open. The official opening wasn't for another thirty minutes, and already a few boys shared they had been there for a couple hours. Even Mir Shir Khan looked eager to start.

Mir Shir Khan placed all the book bags on the floor of the tent. The chalkboard was set up, and he was prepared to give each student a bottle of water when he entered the tent. We surprised him and the students with soccer balls. The kids saw us hand the balls to Mir Shir Khan and were overjoyed. Watching the students jump up and down, Mir Shir Khan looked at me and asked if he could open the school. I laughed, "You're the teacher. You can open whenever you want."

He opened the tent and instructed the students to line up by size. The boys filed in, sitting on the ground as we awaited additional supplies so we could build benches. I looked around at the boys and noticed that only three had shoes. It was hard to imagine these children without shoes, running through jagged stones and sand. I decided as I watched the boys hang on Mir Shir Khan's every word that my next project would be to see if my school back home could have a shoe drive. We observed for a few minutes and left, not wanting to be a distraction.

Over a period of the next three weeks, there were seven more rocket attacks on the base. Three of the attacks came from the east and four from the south and west. We were fortunate not to suffer any serious casualties. Brady called a meeting in the Op center to discuss the attacks and try to come up with a plan to stop them. We knew the weapons were coming out of Pakistan; the question was how they were being transported. The riverbed south of the firebase ran east to west and was a highly traveled route in and out of Pakistan. I suggested that they were being transported right under our noses in the vehicles that pass by the firebase every day. The foot patrols that were going out every night were not having any success in stopping the transfer of weapons across the border.

I made a suggestion: "When I was with the police department, we would target specific crime areas then do vehicle and traffic stops. Once we stopped a vehicle for a moving violation, we would do a consent search, and nine times out of ten, we would come up with some kind of contraband, either drugs or stolen property. We should do the same thing here."

"You mean stop vehicles and search them?" Brady asked.

"That's exactly what I mean. Steve and I have talked about it, and we think that would really disrupt their weapons trafficking."

"That's an interesting idea. How would it work?"

"We would do it just like we did in the police department. We will have a spotter and a couple of chase vehicles. The spotter will identify the vehicle then radio it to the chase vehicles. The chase vehicles will intercept the vehicle and conduct a search. If they are clean, we let them go. If not, we confiscate the weapons and take them back to the firebase."

"I like that idea; I like it a lot. Let's run with it. When do you want to start?"

"Let's start tomorrow. We can put the chase teams and spotter teams together now, and later on, I would like to do some rehearsals with them."

We created four teams. Each team consisted of two gunship chase vehicles with five soldiers and an interpreter in each vehicle, and two spotter teams consisting of two soldiers utilizing our Mercedes SUVs. One spotter team and two chase teams would operate west of the firebase, and the other spotter and chase teams would operate east of the firebase. The spotters would sit on a hilltop where they could get a clear view of their part of the valley. When they spotted a vehicle, they would radio the chase vehicles. That afternoon, we got all the teams together and went down to the range. Each team practiced how it was going to stop a vehicle, and which members of the team would conduct the search and which members would provide security. The teams practiced until they felt confident in their newly acquired skill.

That night, Warren and I talked about building a permanent school building. He found a couple local masons who could build a permanent building. We were going to use some of our operation fund to build it; it was going to cost us about $500. I told Warren that we should build a hard structure for ourselves. It would provide us with a lot more security during a rocket attack. Warren really liked the idea, so we decided to build ourselves a structure, too. We ran the idea past Brady and Ross, and they liked it. We told the local masons that we wanted a building built for ourselves along with the school. They said they were happy to build us one and would start on it in a couple of days.

The next day, we began our vehicle and traffic patrol. I was on one chase team, and Steve was on another. We patrolled up and down the dry riverbed for a while, then we would sit and watch. It was about thirty minutes into the patrol when the spotter observed a vehicle cross the border from Pakistan into Afghanistan. We sat and watched it approach. Spycher was in one gunship, and I was in the other. As the vehicle approached, I could see it was a large Kamaz jingle truck.

A Kamaz was a Russian-made delivery truck, about the size of an Army deuce and a half cargo truck. We called them "jingle trucks," because the Afghans would decorate their vehicles with all kinds of beads and hanging decorations. They were decorated so much that it reminded me of a gaudy Christmas tree. When they drove their vehicles, all their decorations would jingle, hence "jingle trucks."

Spycher pulled out in front of the vehicle, and I pulled in behind it, just as we practiced. I radioed the firebase that we were stopping a vehicle and what our location was. The soldier in the turret manning the .50 caliber in Spycher's vehicle motioned for the driver to stop his vehicle. When the vehicle stopped, the soldier trained the .50 caliber on him. Our vehicle stopped behind the Kamaz and took up a defensive position. The soldiers in both vehicles exited the gunships and set up a 360-degree perimeter around the vehicle, just as we had practiced. Spycher and I, along with Naime, walked up to the driver. We had Naime explain to the driver what we were doing and that we needed to search his vehicle. The driver was very accommodating and opened up the rear doors to his truck. The soldiers who were designated as the search team came up and did a thorough search of the vehicle. I directed them where to search, making sure they looked under the vehicle as well.

The driver was clean; we thanked him for his patience and let him go. Everyone seemed a little disappointed that we didn't find anything. I told them we might search a dozen vehicles before we find something. I had the same results when I did the searches for the police department, I told them. We did three more searches that day, and each one had the same result: nothing found. The other three teams performed searches also, with the same results.

The next day, we were back out there patrolling. It was about 1:30 P.M., and we had performed one search about two hours earlier. The day before, there was more traffic crossing the border. Steve's team radioed that they were stopping a Kamaz just east of the firebase. They had been out with the vehicle for about five minutes when he radioed me to respond to his location—they needed some assistance with the search. When we pulled up, Steve came over to me and said, "You have got to see this." We walked over to the back of the truck, and underneath a pile of rugs were fifteen cases of 60-mm mortar rounds and several dozen 107-mm rockets. Steve radioed back to the firebase with what they had found.

Brady and Mauldin came down to the scene.

"You guys were right; this is how they are transporting the weapons."

I knew we had just scored some big points with Brady.

"That's what we figured; it just took a little police intuition."

We drove the truck back to the firebase and unloaded it. Brady and Mauldin took the driver to the Op center and interviewed him. He said he didn't know what he was carrying; he was just paid to drive the vehicle from Pakistan to Gayan. He was to wait in Gayan for further instructions. Brady asked him who was going to give him those instructions, and he said he didn't know—just that someone in a black SUV would find him. It was obvious he was lying. Brady sent a SITREP to Bagram about what we found and that we had a PUC that needed to be picked up. There was a resupply scheduled for the next day, and they would pick the PUC up then. We continued to run the V & T operation two to three times per week for the remainder of our time at Lwara. We intercepted four more weapon caches that were being transported across the border from Pakistan to Afghanistan during that time period.

Warren had radio duty, so Steve and I ran a team meeting that night to discuss our success with the V & T operation. Warren and Roger were busy planning the construction of our new quarters and school while Steve, Tim, Fred, and I worked on the operation. Brady was thrilled with the success of our operation. He wanted to incorporate us into all operations. From now on, anytime a patrol left the firebase, he wanted one of our team members to be on the patrol. I explained to the team that we had come a long way in earning their respect and that they now want us to be a part of all their operations says a lot about our ability to perform our mission. I wanted them all to know that I was very proud of them. Everyone was happy with what had been accomplished so far. Just then, Warren came walking into the tent.

He said, "I've got some news. The Army is opening up three new firebases, and they need three more CA teams for those bases. Roger, Fred, and myself are to leave for Bagram on the next resupply. They will organize the new teams then send them out. Mike, you are now the new team leader."

I wasn't really surprised; I had heard that they were planning on opening up more firebases. I knew when that happened, they would create new teams, but I figured I would be the one to leave. I was glad I was staying here, and especially that they were leaving Tim and Steve with me. We had a real strong team. I would find out later that Brady and Ross found out about the changes, and they requested that Steve and I stay. The resupply was scheduled for the next day, so Warren, Roger, and Fred spent the rest of the night packing.

"INCOMING, INCOMING, INCOMING." I jumped up just as the roar went over the tent. Another attack. I was getting good at this, and it took me less than a minute to get my gear and take cover in the bunker. The flash and explosion—it landed in the LZ again. The FLIR was trying to get a fix on the launch position. "INCOMING, INCOMING, INCOMING." I listened for the rocket, then the flash and a tremendous explosion; the ground shook violently, then another flash and explosion. My ears were ringing. I could smell something that smelled like a hot, metallic odor. I couldn't tell what it was. Then there was a series of violent explosions coming from the back of the base. Another flash and another explosion, and this time it came from the front of the base. I could still smell that strange odor. Finally, the FLIR had a fix and the mortars went into action. They fired three rounds and were told to cease fire. I looked out, and there was fire all over the camp. Several tents were on fire, and the ammo bunker took a direct hit. The FLIR called out and said two A-10s were one minute out. The FLIR locked on the position from which the rockets were fired, then the A-10s made a bombing run. They dropped two five-hundred-pound bombs on the site. There was a huge explosion and then, about ten seconds later, we could feel the concussion; everyone cheered.

The rockets that were fired at us were white phosphorus incendiary rockets. White phosphorus is commonly referred to as "WP." The slang term "Willy (i.e.) Pete," dating from World War I, is still used by infantryman to refer to white phosphorus. It was against the Geneva Convention to use white phosphorus against open troops, but we were not fighting an army that recognized the Geneva Convention. We were fighting terrorists, and they didn't follow any rules. White phosphorus was designed for use as a flare and smoke-producing agent. The primary use of white phosphorus munitions is to create smokescreens to mask movement from the enemy or to mask his fire. In contrast to other smoke-causing munitions, WP burns quickly, causing an instant bank of smoke. However, white phosphorus has a secondary effect. White phosphorus burns quite fiercely and can set cloth, fuel, ammunition, and other combustibles on fire. It also can function as an antipersonnel weapon, with the compound capable of causing serious burns or death. The agent is used in bombs, artillery, and mortars, and short-range missiles that burst into burning flakes of phosphorus on impact.

It took an hour to put out all the fires, and several tents were destroyed along with our ammo bunker. All the tents received some sort of damage. Sleeping bags and cots were burned; many soldiers lost uniforms and spare boots. Brady called in an emergency resupply to replace the ammo that was lost. Another attack, and it was now obvious that our enemy would do anything to inflict casualties. Still, there were no serious injuries, and I wasn't sure how long our luck would last.

The resupply helicopter landed, and Warren, Roger, and Fred got on it and headed back to Bagram. Warren would start a new team in Gardez with Fred and Roger.

This is our team picture at the front gate of Firebase Lwara. We are the five soldiers standing in front of the Humvee. I'm standing in the middle with our interpreter, Naime, to my left. The other soldiers in the picture are members of the 82nd airborne.

Here I am holding a Jurga at firebase Lwara. I am in the center with the white baseball cap.

This was just some of the weapons and munitions that we found when we raided Bakka Jan's residence.

Here we are negotiating with the Pakistan border guards. We were on our way to intercept the insurgents firing at the firebase. The border guards had moved their checkpoint west into Afghanistan. Naime is behind me telling me what they are saying.

This is Firebase Lwara after we pulled out and it was destroyed.

This was one of the trails that ran along the mountains in Madr Valley. The locals would use these trails to move along the mountains.

Here I am meeting with the elder from Do Sakh. He is the one with the white turban. I don't have a happy look because the elder just served us yogurt.

12

Gayan II

I got word from Bagram that Mir Shir Khan's son was going to be transferred to a civilian hospital in Kabul. He ended up losing both legs, but they were able to save his arm. I got the okay to put Mir Shir Khan on the next resupply helicopter. He could accompany his son when they transferred him to the Kabul hospital, then fly back to Lwara the following week. I drove down to the school to give him the news. He was so excited about visiting his son, he asked me if his other two sons could go with him, I told him sure; they will have plenty of room for them. I found out that the hospital they were sending his son to would make him prosthetic devices for his legs. Mir Shir Khan was very appreciative. We talked about the school, and I told him the school I worked for in the United States had conducted a school supplies collection for his school. On his return from Kabul, the supplies should be here.

He had twenty-five kids attending school, all boys. The elders told us the girls could come, but they never showed up. Mir Shir Khan was going to close the school while he was gone, but Naime volunteered to run it for him. He didn't like missing any time, but he really wanted to see his son; he was glad that Naime was going to help him out. I told him that, hopefully, we could start building the permanent school soon. We had all the supplies; we were just waiting on the local masons. He agreed it would be very nice to have the permanent building with more room.

Our new building was almost done. It had been three weeks since they started it; all that was left was to put on the roof. It would provide us with a lot of protection. The walls were eighteen inches thick and made of sun-dried earthen bricks, the same type of bricks used on the compound walls. These walls were very strong; the compound walls had taken a direct hit from a 107-mm rocket, and the rocket didn't penetrate them. Once the building was completed, we couldn't move in until all the bricks had dried, which would take five days.

Ross called Steve and me to the Op center. He and Brady wanted to pay a visit to the Pakistan border guards at Lwara. Brady also wanted to get a look at Lwara and take some pictures. We couldn't go in the village, because it was in Pakistan, but we could get a clear view of it from the border. The SOT-A team had been picking up a lot of radio chatter coming out of Lwara. The border guards were not part of the active Pakistan military. They were equivalent to our National Guard. They wore the Pakistan military uniform, but their loyalties were with the tribal elders and not with the President of Pakistan. Our AO border was the tribal region of Waziristan, part of the FATA (Federally Administered Tribal Area) of Pakistan. The FATA stretches five hundred miles along the Afghan border. For centuries, this area has been lawless, violent, and remote. It is a breeding ground for Jihad. The Taliban and Al-Qaeda militants were using this area as a launching pad for attacks on American bases along the border. The tribes of Waziristan were strong supporters of the Taliban, and these tribes played a large part in the Taliban's rise to power in Afghanistan. With the border guards supporting the tribal elders of Waziristan, Taliban forces were able to cross the border unchecked. Ross wanted to do a show of force at the border.

"We want to let them know whom they're playing with," Ross said. He wanted everyone to wear all their gear, including their helmets. We usually just wore baseball caps when we went out on patrol. We were going to take twenty soldiers and four gunships.

It was about a ten-minute ride to the border checkpoint. As we pulled up, we could tell that we surprised the guards. They were sitting together in the shade of a juniper tree. They jumped and ran for their positions. There were two guards manning a machine gun on each side of the checkpoint, two guards checking vehicles, and a fifth guard who was the officer in charge. He was on his radio, telling somebody about our arrival. He was making a lot of hand gestures and shrugging his shoulders. It looked like he was arguing with the person on the other end of the radio. Our vehicles took up a defensive position, and the soldiers with us exited their vehicles and took up defensive positions around the checkpoint. Steve and I walked up to the officer in charge and shook his hand. Ross wanted me to do the talking so Brady and Ross could wander around and get a look at Lwara.

The checkpoint was only a few hundred yards from the entrance to Lwara. It was a small village with seven or eight buildings lining the road that ran through it. We shook hands with him, and I had Naime tell him what we were doing here. We told him we were new to the area, and we wanted to see where the border was. He wouldn't make eye contact with us; when he shook our hands, he looked to the ground. Steve and I looked at each other; we were both thinking the same thing—everyone in this country has something to hide. As we stood there and talked to him, Brady and Ross walked up on a knoll to get a better look at Lwara. There were several antennas mounted on the rooftops throughout the village. As Ross looked through his binoculars, he could see several armed men standing on one of the buildings looking at us. I told the officer in charge that I would like to get a picture of him and me standing together. I had Steve take our picture. I really didn't want a picture of him—we wanted pictures of the checkpoint and Lwara, but we didn't want him to know that was what we wanted. We stood with our backs to the checkpoint, and Steve took several pictures of the checkpoint and the village. The last picture he took was the two of us. We had a digital camera, so Steve walked up to the guard and showed him the picture of the two of us. He smiled and said he liked it. We walked over to the other guards and took their pictures. Steve did the same thing as he did with the officer. By the time we finished, Steve got fifty good pictures of the checkpoint and Lwara, and the guards never knew it. When we got back to the firebase, we reviewed the pictures with Brady and Ross.

"There is a lot of activity going on in Lwara," Ross said.

"I counted six antennas throughout the village; no wonder SOT-A is picking up so much radio chatter," added Brady.

"The officer in charge didn't like us being there; he sure was nervous," I said.

"He sure was. I just wish we could get in the village."

"So do I, but that is not going to happen," Ross interjected.

"We need to observe that checkpoint and see what is going on."

"Good idea. I'll get with Spycher and have him set something up." We were sure that all the weapons coming across the border came through that checkpoint. Brady and Ross wanted to know what was going on during the night. Spycher could have a team set up and observe it with their NVGs (Night Vision Goggles).

We finally moved into our new building. It was so much bigger and better than the tent. We went up to the bazaar in Arghamel and bought some rugs and a water heater. We were able to piece enough wood together to build a table and storage bins for each of us. With Warren, Roger, and Fred gone now, we had some extra room. On the last resupply mission, the 20th Group sent two CI (Counter Intelligence) soldiers, Brett and Carl, to the base to assist with the intelligence gathering. We invited them to stay in our building. They couldn't believe how lucky they were to stay with us. The building with the rugs, television, and furniture made our conditions a little more bearable. Everyone on the base wanted to hang out at our hooch.

We had been eating MREs and T-Rats for so long now that everyone was really sick of them. One day Brady had been out on patrol with his team, and when they returned, they had a cow with them. He said they were on patrol when they came across a group of nomads. The nomads had several different animals with them, one of them being a cow. Brady ended up buying the cow from them. He gave them ten dollars for it. He said, "We're going to butcher it and have a big cookout." This cow wasn't the typical cow that we have in the United States. This was the skinniest thing I had ever seen.

"It's a little skinny, don't you think, Brady?" I asked.

"Ya, I know, we will just have to fatten him up," Brady replied.

"What do you plan on feeding him? There's not a lot of grass around here."

"He can eat MREs just like the rest of us."

"I've never seen a cow eat an MRE before, but then again, I've never tried to feed one an MRE." Brady had one of his guys take the cow to one of the empty tents, and there it stayed for the next week. The cow liked the pound cake and the jelly and crackers. Every day when someone got a pound cake or jelly and crackers in his MRE, he would toss it in the tent for the cow. After six days, I went in the tent to check on the cow. He wasn't getting fatter; as a matter of fact, I thought he was skinnier than before. Brady came walking in while I was looking at the cow. He agreed it was getting skinnier.

The next day was Friday, so Brady decided it was time to butcher him. One of the soldier's on Brady's team worked in his parent's meat store in Texas, and he knew how to butcher the cow. The next morning, we had a resupply, and to our amazement Bagram sent us a case of T-bone steaks. There were forty steaks in the case, not enough for everyone, so our cook decided to mix those in with the steaks we were going to get from the cow.

That afternoon, there was an excitement around the base that I had never seen before. Everyone was so excited about eating a steak. The cow was taken down to the LZ and butchered. They got several steaks out of him. Back on the firebase, we dug a barbeque pit and grilled both the cow steaks and the steaks we got from Bagram. The cook had mixed all the steaks together in a big pan. We all lined up outside the mess tent, anxiously waiting for the tent flap to open. Finally it was ready, and we filed through the tent. The servers took a steak out of the pan and put it on our plates, and we got a spoonful of corn. We all walked back to our tent to eat.

The steak smelled so good I couldn't wait to eat it. We all sat down. Steve and Tim were the first ones to get a bite. They said it was the best steak they ever had. I took out my knife and attempted to cut a piece off. I cut, and cut, and cut and finally got a piece off. I put it in my mouth, and it was the most terrible steak I had ever tasted. It was like trying to eat a rubber eraser, and it tasted like one. I looked over to Tim and Steve, and they were devouring their steaks. I realized what happened. They got the steaks from Bagram, and I got one from the Afghan cow. I was so mad; I wanted that steak so bad. Tim and Steve thought it was real funny. I suppose I would have found it funny, too, if it had been one of them who got the Afghan cow steak. No one could eat the Afghan cow steaks, so forty lucky soldiers that day got the good steaks, and the rest of us ate a MREs.

It had been nearly two months since our last raid on Bakka Jan's compound. Brady got word that there was a large weapons cache stored there. His informant was looking to make money from the offer Brady made at the Jurga whereby he would pay for information and recovery of a weapons cache. His informant told him exactly where it was and how much was there. It was a large cache consisting of mortars, rockets, and machine guns. We didn't have much time, because Bakka Jan's men were going to move it again in two days. We worked together in creating an operations plan for a Cordon Search. This time we were going to move in under the cover of darkness, and we wouldn't have the support of the F-16s. We were to leave the firebase at 2:00 A.M. and convoy to Gayan under blackout conditions; all the lights on the vehicles would be turned off, and the driver would use his NVGs to navigate. We would move to a designated staging area just outside of Gayan and wait until first light. At 6:15, Brady would give the order to execute the search, and the units would move in.

Brady wanted Steve and me to be on the search team this time. He wanted to use our experience in conducting searches for the police departments. I had Tim lead the blocking force at the intersection. Going in as early as we were, we should be in and out before anyone knew what was going on. I didn't anticipate a large crowd gathering at the intersection as it did the last time.

We passed through the front gate at 2:30 A.M., just as planned. Everyone who was involved in the raid last time was going on this mission. This was the first mission for Brett and Carl, and they rode in our vehicle. Steve drove, and I had the front passenger seat. I had used the NVGs for training purposes in the past, but this was my first time using them on a combat mission. NVGs magnify the ambient light, allowing us to see in the dark. Everything is green, and there is no depth perception. Steve was finding it difficult to follow the vehicle in front of him; he nearly ran into the back of it several times. We drove at a very slow pace. It took nearly two hours to get to the staging area, located on a hilltop about a quarter mile from the intersection leading to Bakka Jan's residence. We took up a defensive position and waited for Brady to give the order to begin the raid.

When we got to the staging area, I exited the vehicle and took up a defensive position on some large rocks next to the vehicle. I had a perfect view of Gayan. It was eerily quiet as we waited for the order to move out. Occasionally, I could hear the tap of a finger on a chewing tobacco can as a soldier was packing the tobacco for a chew. It was a new moon, so it was very dark—perfect conditions for a nighttime movement. At 5:30 A.M., Brady gave the order to commence the raid. It was a fast ride from the staging area to the compound. Steve and I were to assist with security outside while the compound was cleared. We would then enter and assist with the search. As we arrived, everyone took up his position. Steve pulled our vehicle across the road that led past the compound, blocking any vehicles that might come down the road; he then went over to Spycher's vehicle, about three hundred feet east of my position.

The breech team placed a C-4 charge on the big steel doors and blew them open. The clearing teams then entered the compound and began clearing it. They were looking for anyone who might be in the compound. If they found someone, they would handcuff him and place him in a holding area in the compound. I could hear some yelling coming from inside the compound; I figured they must have found someone in there.

As I waited for the word to go in, I heard something coming down the road. I couldn't tell what it was, but I knew it wasn't a vehicle. The sun was just starting to come up, and I strained to see what it was. Finally, it got close enough to see. It was a man walking a camel. I motioned for the man to stop. Naime was with Steve. I radioed to Steve to send Naime over to me. The man stood there patiently holding on to the camel. Naime came over, and I had him tell the man he wasn't going to be able to pass by until we were done here; it might be an hour or so. Naime talked with him. He said the man was on his way to Pakistan, and he and his camel would rest on the side of the road until he could leave. It was then I found out what nasty a disposition camels have. The man stood there patiently waiting, but his camel was a different story. The camel would grunt and blat then spit at me. The man would try to calm him down, but the camel didn't want any part of it. He would pull away and thrash his head, then he would grunt, blat, and spit again. I was getting really annoyed with this animal. I was trying to focus and concentrate on what was happening, but he kept distracting me with all his grunting, blatting, and spitting. Finally, I got the word the compound was clear and to move in to assist with the search. I was really glad to get away from that camel. One of the 82nd soldiers came over to relieve me, and I told him "good luck" with it.

As I entered the compound, I saw four individuals sitting in the center, their hands handcuffed behind their backs. Brady told me that they were found hiding in one of the rooms. We began searching the compound. There was a pile of juniper branches in one corner of the compound. Steve pulled some of the branches back and found six cases of 60-mm mortar rounds. Mauldin was searching one of the rooms in the compound when he found a false floor under a mattress. He lifted it up and found the rest of the weapons cache. There were two dozen rockets, three cases of Russian hand grenades, ten more cases of mortar rounds, and several cases of AK-47 ammunition. This was the largest weapons cache recovery to date. Making the offer of paying for information on weapons caches was now starting to pay off. It also helped that we were providing some humanitarian relief. We were sticking by our promise of helping the villages, thus gaining the support of the elders. We knew we couldn't win everybody over, but at least it was a start.

We were putting a crimp on the weapons trafficking throughout the valley. All vehicles that came in and out of Pakistan were searched; we had patrols out at night, and we had a successful raid on Bakka Jan's compound. SOT-A was picking up a lot of radio chatter indicating a large-scale attack on a U.S. firebase. They couldn't determine which base it would be. Firebase Shkin was about fifty miles south of us, and firebase Orgun was twenty miles west. Both firebases had seen an increase in attacks over the past month. Brady and Ross were working their informants, but they weren't getting any information. Tension was running very high around the base. The local workers were much quieter than usual. Everyone knew something big was going to happen; we just didn't know when.

It was 10:00 P.M., and we just finished watching a movie. Steve and I were going to walk over to the Op center. I needed to send out our SITREP for the day, and Steve wanted to talk with Mauldin. Just as we started to go out the door, the air horn went off, "INCOMING, INCOMING, INCOMING," and we hit the ground. I could hear a rocket screaming overhead, and it landed in the LZ with a loud explosion. We jumped up, grabbed our gear, and headed to our fighting positions. Now that we were down to three members on our team, we each had our own fighting position. "INCOMING, INCOMING, INCOMING," another rocket went screaming overhead. At the same time, there was an explosion on the east side of the firebase, and another explosion toward the front of the firebase. Then four more rockets screamed overhead. They were being launched from two different directions.

I could hear gunfire off in the distance. Spycher's team was on observation patrol when they stumbled upon a group of insurgents attempting to fire rockets at the base. Now his team was in a fierce firefight with that group.

The soldier manning the FLIER yelled, "I've got three vehicles approaching the firebase at a high rate of speed." Just then, the AMF at the rear of the firebase began shooting. I saw an RPG (rocket propelled grenade) shoot across the back of the firebase.

The FLIER yelled, "The vehicles have stopped, they are setting up a mortar tube." I put on my NVGs and moved over to the side of the Hesco barrier to get a better look. Just as I looked over the barrier, I saw an insurgent with an RPG about thirty feet in front of me. He fired the RPG at me; the flash from his back blast was magnified by the NVGs, and it was like looking directly at a flashbulb. The grenade hit the Hesco barrier right next to my head. The blast knocked me down. I was stunned, the concussion was deafening, and now my ears were ringing and I was seeing spots from the RPG flash. I regained my composure and returned fire.

We were taking small arms fire from all around the base. There were tracer rounds and RPGs flying overhead, and there were explosions from the RPGs impacting the barriers all around. There was a large explosion behind me, and one of their mortar rounds impacted close to one of the fighting positions. I ran over to the fighting position to check on their condition. They were stunned but all right.

Brady radioed Bagram that the base was under attack and requested close air support. Two F-16s were dispatched. The FLIER gave our mortar section the location where the insurgents were firing their mortars from, and our mortar section returned fire. The battle continued to rage, and the insurgents were not withdrawing. The word came down for the mortar section to cease fire; the F-16s were on station. As I looked to the sky with my NVGs, I was able to see the laser designator beaming down from the jet. The F-16s dropped two laser-designated five-hundred-pound bombs. The valley erupted in a massive explosion and fireball, then two more bombs were dropped. Spycher's team was pinned down on a ridge northeast of the firebase. The F-16s then concentrated their effort on providing Spycher's team with close air support. Finally, the insurgents withdrew back across the border. The battle lasted about forty-five minutes, although while we were fighting, it seemed to go on for a longer time. Again, there were no serious injuries; four soldiers received minor shrapnel wounds. Spycher's team made it back unscathed.

We estimated that between 50 and 75 insurgents had attacked the firebase. This was the first time they attempted a coordinated attack on the base. One thing was certain: the attacks were becoming more violent, and the insurgents were becoming more brazen. It was becoming harder to defend the firebase because of its close proximity to Pakistan. It was fairly obvious that the insurgents had the support of the border guards, allowing them to slip back and forth across the border.

After everything quieted down, we met in the Op center to discuss what happened and what the future plans would be. It was determined that we needed more patrols out at night. The problem was that we didn't have enough personnel. Brady was going to put in a request for more soldiers to help with security. We were going to be limited on what CA missions we could do; we didn't have enough soldiers to provide a security detail during the day, because everyone would be tied up at night, running patrols. I would add to my SITREP that we were becoming limited on what CA missions we could do because of the deteriorating stability in the Lwara Valley.

13
Thanksgiving

The attacks on the firebase now were becoming almost a daily occurrence. The Army decided to reinforce the firebase by sending us an LRS (Long Range Surveillance) team. The mission of a LRS team was to infiltrate deep into enemy territory, construct a hide site, and provide continuous surveillance of an area. The teams typically remain in place for up to five days, depending on food and water supplies. The LRS was a ten-member team commanded by Captain Hartwick. As soon as they arrived, Brady, Ross, and Hartwick began planning on where to set up the surveillance teams. They made a decision on where to place the teams, and they immediately moved to those areas. With the LRS conducting the surveillance, the nightly foot patrols could now focus on patrolling.

We received word from Bagram that the Pakistan military wanted to meet with us to discuss the recent attacks. Major Sullivan, an Intelligence Officer with the 20th Group stationed in Bagram, would be joining us for the meeting. Sullivan arrived the day before the meeting on a special flight from Bagram. At our meeting that night in the Op center, Sullivan briefed us on the purpose of the meeting. He said that the Untied States had been putting pressure on Pakistan to get their military involved in cracking down on the Taliban activity in the tribal area. We were going to be meeting with Colonel Mustaffa, an active duty colonel stationed in Islamabad. We would be discussing our concerns about the border guards and the recent insurgent border incursion. Sullivan told us that Pakistan did not have control of their tribal area, but Colonel Mustaffa would probably try to convince us that they do. That was why Sullivan was here—so he could report back to Bagram what the Pakistan military was trying to sell us. Sullivan also told us that, for this meeting, we were to wear our rank. We wanted to let Colonel Mustaffa know with whom he was meeting. Since Sullivan and I were both majors, we would be the ones talking to the colonel. Brady and Ross would be interested bystanders.

The meeting was to take place on a hilltop about a quarter mile west of the border checkpoint. We were taking four vehicles (our SUV and three gunships) and a security element of twelve soldiers. We arrived at the meeting location and were surprised to see that the colonel brought a security element of about one hundred soldiers with him. There were a table and chairs set up in the center of the meeting area, and behind it a small tent. The colonel greeted us and introduced himself and two of his staff officers; we in turn did the same. He invited us to sit at the table. He thanked us for coming, then he motioned to one of the soldiers standing next to the tent. The soldier looked inside, then four soldiers came out of the tent carrying cold Pepsis and gave us each one. The colonel held his up as in a toast and told us to enjoy. It was the first time in three months that I had a Pepsi or anything cold to drink. It was the best Pepsi I had ever drunk.

The colonel started out by telling us how Pakistan is our partner in the war on terror. His government has directed the Pakistan military forces to seek out and destroy Taliban and Al-Qaeda forces that are operating in the tribal border region. We told the colonel that his first order of business should be to find out why the border guards are letting those forces cross the border unchecked. He said he was unaware this was happening and that he would look into it. We talked about the tribal region and some of the information we were gathering coming out of Pakistan. When we were in Bagram, we had briefings on Pakistan and how the government had little control of what went on in the tribal area; listening to the colonel talk reinforced that information. He assured us that they would be assisting us on their side of the border.

We had been talking with the colonel for about thirty minutes when he motioned to one of this soldiers again. This time, he came out of the tent with a plate of french fries and another Pepsi for each of us. Sullivan and I looked at each other; we knew that the colonel was playing a little psychological operation on us. He was hoping that by giving us the fries and Pepsi, we would believe everything he told us and would see him as our ally. The fries and Pepsi were great, but his little game didn't work. We knew he was just giving us lip service and that he was sent here to try to pacify us. We thanked the colonel for meeting with us and looked forward to his support in the war on terror. Sullivan was to return to Bagram on the next resupply. He would report that we met with the Pakistan military, and they told us the military would be conducting combat operations on Taliban and Al-Qaeda forces in the Tribal region, but they gave us no details on how and when.

The resupply arrived and Sullivan got on the helicopter; getting off the helicopter was Major Ronald Benson. He was a psychologist attached to Task Force 180 in Bagram. The Army decided to send him out to our firebase to check on our morale. Someone in Bagram was concerned that maybe our morale was starting to deteriorate due to all of the attacks on the firebase. Benson was a reservist from Indianapolis. He was fifty-three years old, tall, thin, and had grey hair. He wore glasses that were too big for his thin face. He had been out of the military for nearly fifteen years, but after September 11th, he decided to get back in and finish his twenty years. We invited him to stay in our hooch. He said he would be here until the next resupply, so he would be spending Thanksgiving with us. At our nightly briefing in the Op center, Benson told us that he was here just to see how things were going with everyone and that, if anybody felt the need to talk with him, he would be available. Brady seemed a little annoyed with the whole thing, but since he was staying with us, he didn't care.

His indoctrination to life in a forward operating base didn't take very long. We had another rocket attack that night. We had become used to them now; they weren't as traumatic anymore, but that wasn't the case for Benson. He was definitely shaken up from the experience. Just as we had been welcomed to the firebase by Thompson after our first attack, I welcomed Benson.

Over the next few days, we visited a couple of the villages and distributed more humanitarian aid. Benson went along with us; he wanted to get a feel of what our day-to-day activities were. Brady and Ross had their teams running patrols every night. Mauldin and two of the SOT-A soldiers joined our team, and we became daytime patrol. The attacks had shifted from the east and now were coming form the north and west. The addition of the LRS team and the constant patrols of the two A-teams forced the insurgents to use different tactics.

It was Thanksgiving, and on the menu was T-Rat lasagna. The day was really no different from any other day. We had received another rocket attack the night before. This time it came from north of the firebase. The soldier manning the FLIER spotted five individuals running from the launch site. There were some compounds in the area that the individuals ran toward. Brady wanted me to take my team out and check the area and the compounds for any evidence.

Mauldin, Carl, the counterintelligence soldier, and Benson joined Tim, Steve, and me on the patrol. We had our Mercedes SUV and a gunship with the Mark-19. We headed out the back gate and made our way toward the suspected launch site. We were about five miles from the firebase when we came upon the first compound. Tim was in the gunship manning the Mark-19. Benson and Carl assisted with perimeter security, and Mauldin, Steve, and I searched the compound. The place was deserted; it appeared that nobody had been here in quite awhile. We found some spent casings from an AK-47, but that was it. We drove over to another compound about a half mile away, but that, too, was empty. We checked three more compounds that were also empty. In the last compound we checked, we found tire tracks and fresh footprints. The tire tracks came from the direction of Wrice. We searched around the area and, about one hundred yards south of the compound, we found the launch site. Inside the compound, we found some wire that they used to attach the rockets to a firing device. Steve radioed into the firebase with what we found.

It was 1:30, and we were hungry, so we decided to park the vehicles on one of the hilltops and eat an MRE. There were a couple more compounds north that we wanted to check before we headed back to the firebase. We all got out an MRE and used the hood of the vehicles as our table.

"What a great way to spend Thanksgiving," I said.

"Well, it's either this or spend time with my in-laws, and I think I'd rather be here," replied Carl. We all laughed.

"They can't be that bad."

"You ain't never met my mother-in-law. Believe me, if you had, you'd rather be here, too." Carl went on to tell us some stories from previous Thanksgivings he had spent with his in-laws. He kept us laughing for quite awhile. Then all of us started taking turns telling Thanksgiving stories.

We had been there for about forty minutes when we heard an explosion off in the distance, coming from the vicinity of the firebase. A minute later, another explosion. We then got a radio message from Brady that the firebase was under attack and that the rockets fired at the base came from the ruins. The "ruins" was a name we gave to an abandoned village that sat on a hill just south of the border checkpoint. There wasn't much left of the buildings—just a few walls. We were the only unit out on patrol, and we could get to the ruins fast and engage those who were shooting at the firebase.

From where we were, it was about a five-minute drive to the ruins. We headed southeast across the rolling hills. We were headed for the dry riverbed that ran past the firebase to the border checkpoint. Just as we crested the hill next to the riverbed, we had to slam on our brakes. I couldn't believe what was in front of us. The Pakistan border guards had moved the checkpoint about a quarter of a mile into Afghanistan, and now we just came up behind them. I don't know who was more surprised, them or us. We skidded to a stop; they turned around and pointed their guns at us. There were two guards to our left who were manning a machine gun, and they trained that on us. They were yelling at each other, and the officer in charge was redirecting his soldiers to focus on us. There must have been ten guards there, whereas they usually only had four at the checkpoint. I could see that one of the guards was making a call on his radio. Mauldin, Steve, Naime, and I exited our vehicles and walked up to the officer in charge. Mauldin and the officer in charge began yelling at each other. Mauldin was yelling at him in English, and the officer was yelling at Mauldin in Pashtu. I looked at Tim and told him to put the Mark-19 on the two manning the machine gun. Naime began translating for Mauldin. The officer was telling us that we had entered Pakistan illegally.

"Bullshit, this is Afghanistan. You can't move your checkpoint," Mauldin yelled.

"This is Pakistan, and you are in violation."

"I'll tell you what, our firebase is being shot at from that hill, and we are going to go through you whether you like it our not."

"You cannot go through here."

"Watch us!"

We got back in our vehicles and drove through the checkpoint. They weren't happy; we drove over their barrier as they were yelling at us. I couldn't believe that they moved the checkpoint into Afghanistan. They must have been there as a lookout for the ones shooting at the firebase. We headed down the riverbed then up the hill toward the ruins. We stopped just before we entered the ruins. We placed the gunship in an overwatch position then slowly made our way in. It didn't take long to clear the area; we found the location where they were launching the rockets. We could see several different sets of footprints, but the attackers were long gone.

We were just getting ready to radio the firebase that it was all clear when we heard two helicopters off in the distance. As we listened, we could tell that they were coming our way. I asked Mauldin if we were expecting a resupply, and he said no. We finally got a visual on them; it was a Blackhawk and an Apache. I radioed the firebase to see if they were expecting them, and they said no. As I watched the helicopters, I couldn't believe what I saw. The Blackhawk landed right in front of the real border checkpoint, five soldiers jumped out and ran into the building next to the checkpoint, and then the Blackhawk took off. Several vehicles began to converge on the checkpoint. The vehicles were full of border guards. As I watched, more and more vehicles kept arriving. There must have been close to seventy-five guards there now. They surrounded the building where the five soldiers had entered. I looked at Mauldin and told him we needed to go down there and help them. We had just pissed those guys off by running through their checkpoint, now we have got to go back down there and try to rescue these soldiers, and we don't even know who they are or why they are here.

I radioed back to the firebase and told them what was going on and for them to send the QRF to our location. Brady said he would try and find out who they were. The Blackhawk and Apache continued to circle the area. We made our way down the hill and over to the checkpoint. All the soldiers in their unit must have been there. There were several vehicles with machine guns on them, and they were all pointed at us. The commander of the unit came over to us. We had never met him before. He introduced himself. He wanted to know why we were violating the border agreement and why we sent our combat forces into Pakistan without authorization. I told him there must have been a mistake and that we didn't intentionally do that. I asked him if I could speak with the soldiers. He told me that they were his prisoners. I again asked him if I could speak with them and try to clear this up. He finally motioned to one of the other guards to open the door and let me in.

The building that the soldiers were in was the barracks for the border guards. When I went inside, the five soldiers were lined up against the back wall. We shook hands and I asked them what was going on. They said they were with the 19th Special Forces Group in Orgun, and they were on a reconnaissance flight when they heard the radio call that firebase Lwara was under attack. They decided to fly over to see if they could help. They spotted four armed individuals running into this building, so they decided to land and go after them. They didn't realize that this was Pakistan and that the armed individuals were actually border guards. I told them to let me go back out and see what I could do.

Brady, Ross, and the QRF just pulled in. I told Brady and Ross what happened. They couldn't believe it. I told the guard commander how it was just a big mistake, and the soldiers in the barracks weren't from our firebase but from Orgun. I explained how our base came under attack, they came to help us, and spotted four armed persons enter the building. They didn't know this was Pakistan and those were guards. The commander didn't want to listen to me. He told me they were his prisoners. Brady made radio contact with the Apache; he had it hovering just above us. He told the commander that we were going to take our soldiers out of there, and if he tried to stop us, the Apache would open up on them. It was very intimidating looking down the barrel of all those weapons on the Apache. Brady motioned for me to go down and get them out of the building. I opened the door and told them to come on. As the Apache hovered, the Blackhawk landed, the five soldiers got back on, and it took off. We got back into our vehicles and headed out. After all the vehicles were out, the Apache took off. My heart was racing; I couldn't believe what I just went through. I thought at any moment we were going to start shooting it out with the border guards. The only thing that saved us was the Apache. The guard commander knew he was outgunned by the Apache, and those five soldiers weren't worth it. Things were already bad. With this incident, I couldn't imagine what was in store for our future.

14

Bugging Out

It seemed to be a revolving door on the resupply. Someone was leaving, and someone new was arriving. Benson had spent a very eventful week with us and was now on his way back to Bagram. Our new arrival was Chaplain Mitch Larson. Chaplain Larson was a tall, lean Texan with a tightly cropped crew cut and a strong handshake. He was the third chaplain to visit the firebase since September, but he was by far the most dynamic. He was not the typical chaplain; he was a former Green Beret. He spent ten years with the 5th Special Forces Group and was a veteran of Desert Storm. He left the Army in 1992 to attend the University of Pittsburg. In 1996, he decided to follow his calling, and he was accepted to the Boston University of Theology. In 1999, he was ordained a Methodist minister. He returned to the Army in 2000 and received a commission as a captain in Chaplain Services.

He held church services that night in the mess tent. When the other chaplains held a service, only four or five soldiers would attend. Not the case for Larson: it was standing room only in the tent. He connected with everyone on the base, because he had been in our shoes. His dynamic personality and storytelling really grabbed your attention. He had been on the firebase for four days when he got talking to Ross about the time he spent with the Green Berets. Ross's team was going out on patrol that night, and Chaplain Larson asked Ross if he could accompany them. Chaplains are noncombatants, so they are not allowed to carry a weapon, but Larson was Special Forces, and Ross didn't think it would hurt to have the chaplain tag along. He knew how to handle himself.

The patrol left the firebase at 9:00 P.M. They were headed to the hill south of the firebase. The LRS teams were set up on the hills west of the firebase. Ross wanted to concentrate on the hills to the south. Two days before, a local came to the firebase to report he found some rockets set up on the hill and pointed toward the firebase. A team was sent out, and they found four rockets attached to a timer. They disarmed and destroyed the rockets. Ross wanted his team to patrol that area.

The patrol had been out for two and a half hours. They were on the backside of the hill, following a trail, when there was an explosion at the rear of the patrol. Chaplain Larson had stepped on an antipersonnel mine. It was a Russian OZM-3 bounding mine, commonly referred to as a "Bouncing Betty." When the mine is tripped, a small propelling charge launches the body of the mine three to four feet into the air, where the main charge bursts and sprays fragmentation waist high. Chaplain Larson received shrapnel wounds to both legs; fortunately, he was wearing a protective vest that protected his back. His wounds were severe enough that a medivac helicopter was dispatched, and Chaplain Larson was evacuated to Bagram. He was stabilized there, then flown to the United States, where he eventually made a full recovery.

The Army was allowing soldiers to take ten days leave during their deployment. I requested to take leave over Christmas, and my request was approved. Steve had also put in for the same time, and his request was approved. Our leave was scheduled to begin on December 22nd in Germany. Steve's wife was a travel agent, so she purchased the plane tickets for us. We were flying from Frankfurt, Germany, to the United States on December 22nd, so we had to begin coordinating our flight from Lwara to Bagram then Bagram to Germany. We wanted to make sure we didn't miss the flight out of Germany. We had a resupply scheduled for December 19th, so Steve and I were going to hop that flight back to Bagram. There was a flight from Bagram to Germany on the 21st, and our team in Bagram booked us on it. We could hardly wait until the 19th; it was going to be a long week.

At our briefing that night, Brady told us he just got the word that the firebase was closing. The Army decided that, because the firebase was so close to Pakistan, we couldn't adequately defend it. We had two days to pack everything up. Brady, Ross, and the 82nd were being sent to Kandahar (they were to convoy there), and the rest of us were flying to Bagram. The base was going to be turned over to the AMF. It was a smart thing to do. We were very fortunate that no one had been killed; it would just be a matter of time if we stayed. Now I wondered where we would be sent next. I wasn't looking forward to starting all over again.

The next two days were crazy. We couldn't tell the locals that we were leaving, but they knew something was up. As we began loading equipment up in the Humvees, it was pretty hard to hide. The attacks on the base didn't let up; we had two attacks one night then another on our last night. It was a fitting way to end our time there.

It was December 16th, our last day in Lwara. The helicopters were picking us up in two hours. Mir Shir Khan came to the firebase to find out what was going on. Mir Shir Khan had become a friend, and it was hard telling him we were leaving. I knew I would never see him again. He was very disappointed, although he understood why. I told him I hoped he would continue on with the school. We were leaving the tent and all the school supplies, plus I told him I would pay him for another month. He told me he loved to teach and that he would keep the school open. He was very grateful for the opportunity we gave him. His son was recovering in Kabul, and he hoped to have him home in a couple of months. We shook hands, and I wished him the best of luck.

The interpreters were going on the convoy to Kandahar. Naime had taken a couple of days off to visit his home in Khost. He left before we found out that we were leaving, and he wasn't due back for another day. I felt badly, but I had no way of getting a hold of him. I later learned that Naime was involved in an attack on American forces in Khost. He was captured and sent to Bagram. It turned out that Naime was not the nice guy that he appeared to be. He was connected to a warlord in Khost who was a ranking member of the Taliban. One of the biggest problems we faced was not knowing whom we could trust.

Our security was set out, and we could hear the helicopters off in the distance. As they got closer, we heard gunshots. The helicopters landed, and the crew chief was in a hurry to get us aboard and to get out of there. We got everything loaded up, the helicopter was powered up, and we took off. A lot had happened to us during the four months that we were there. We were much different now from when we arrived. On our flight back, I remembered back to the day we landed in Bagram and when we saw the soldiers who were getting ready to leave. I remembered their weathered faces and beards and the haunted stares they had. I looked over to Steve and Tim, and they now had that same look.

We were met in Bagram by Sergeant Witchikowski, one of our B-team members. We loaded our gear up on his truck, and he took us over to the CJSOTF compound. I met with our B-team commander, Major Matt Kellogg. We talked about Lwara, and he wanted me to accompany him to the U.S. Embassy in Kabul the next day and give a briefing on the subject. We also talked about our next mission. He said he was sending us to Orgun to assist the CA team there. They had a large AO and could use some help. He was also going to realign some of the teams. There were twelve more soldiers from our unit in Syracuse who had been activated in November and were now here. We were going to be getting another team member, Sergeant Antonino Caporicco. Nino, as we called him, was twenty-two years old and a college student from Syracuse. He had four years experience with the 25th Infantry Division. Nino had jet-black hair, a thick beard, and a dark tan. With his beard and dark tan, he looked just like an Afghan. Nino's goal was to become a police officer someday. He had been with the team in Asadabad. Then, after the reorganization of the teams, he joined us. Tim and Nino would be heading to Orgun on the next resupply, and Steve and I would be joining them when we returned from leave.

The next day, we headed to Kabul. It was a forty-five minute drive from Bagram. I was really uncomfortable with the convoy. All we took were three SUVs. There were no gunships, no rehearsals, and no plans on what to do if we came under fire, and we didn't test fire our weapons. A paved highway ran from Bagram to Kabul. The last four months, all we had to travel on were dry riverbeds. The trip from Bagram to Kabul was uneventful; it was nice to ride on a paved highway. Kabul is the largest city in Afghanistan, with a population of 3.5 million. On the outskirts of the city, vendors were selling bread, fruit, and trinkets. As we drove into the city, the traffic became very heavy. As we came up to the first intersection, it was very chaotic. Cars were beeping their horns, and drivers were yelling at each other. I then realized that the traffic signal wasn't working. I was riding with Kellogg; he said none of the traffic signals worked, because there was no electricity in Kabul.

He said jokingly, "The vehicle with the biggest gun has the right of way." It was a crazy ride through the city; we didn't want to get stopped in traffic, so when traffic stopped, we went around it on the sidewalk. We finally made it to the embassy. I gave the briefing on

Lwara to the CJMOTF (Combined Joint Civil Military Operation Task Force) representatives.

After the briefing, I ran into Major Ben Tompkins. Ben was from our unit in Syracuse. He was originally going to deploy with us but, during the physical, he failed the hearing test. He had to get a waiver before he could deploy. His waiver didn't come through until after we deployed, so he had to wait until the October deployment. Ben and I were good friends back home. He lived close to me, so we would ride to drill together. He was a New York State Correctional Officer in the civilian world. He told me that he was a team leader, and their team was stationed in Kabul. He invited Steve and me to spend the rest of the day with him; he would show us around the city, then we would eat dinner at his place, and he would take us back to Bagram that night. We both eagerly agreed, because there was nothing to do back in our tent at Bagram.

Ben and his team lived four blocks from the U.S. Embassy. I couldn't believe how lucky he was; they were living in an apartment. They had a kitchen, bathroom with running water, their own generator for electricity, the Internet, and a phone, and they each had their own bedroom with a real bed. Ben laughed. He said he was mad when he couldn't deploy with us, but now he was really happy the way it worked out. While we were at his apartment, Ben showed us some Persian rugs he purchased. They were beautiful rugs. He told us he got them in a section of the city called Chicken Street. I really wanted to get one, and he said we could get a really good deal on them. I didn't like the idea of driving around the city by ourselves. Ben told us not to worry, and that he did it all the time. I asked him, "How many times have you been shot at?"

"I haven't been shot at," he replied.

"Once you do, you'll have a different outlook."

"Don't worry. Chicken Street is in a safe part of the city. I go down there a couple times a week."

"What are we going to do for security?"

"We'll take my team sergeant, Randy, to assist us."

"That's only four of us."

"Quit worrying. That area is heavily patrolled by ISAF" (International Security Assistance Force). ISAF is a NATO-led security force, established by the United Nations Security Council, that had the mission of securing Kabul. I really wanted to get a Persian rug, and so did Steve. I asked Steve what he thought. He was a little uncomfortable, too, but we decided to go. It was about a five-block drive from the apartment to Chicken Street. The street was lined with stores on both sides. There were all types of stores—rug stores, antique stores, and clothing stores. Each store had a little portable generator on the sidewalk in front of it. The store owners stood in front of their stores and tried to convince us to come inside. It was like walking down the midway of a carnival with all the carnival workers trying to get you to play their game. The street and sidewalk were packed with people. We parked in front of the rug store; Randy provided security outside the store for us. We got a lot of stares from people walking up and down the street. Ben was right; ISAF was patrolling the street, but I still had an uneasy feeling. Randy pulled security outside the store while the three of us went in. The shop owner knew Ben, and he was happy to see him. Ben introduced us, and he told the shop owner we were here to buy some rugs. Steve and I found the rugs we wanted. We bartered with the shop owner and, like Ben said, we got a good price on the rugs. We went back to Ben's apartment and ate dinner, then he gave us a ride back to Bagram.

Ben had it easy living in an apartment with all those comforts, and here we were living in a forward operating base. Our worlds couldn't be more different. I didn't like Kabul, and I wouldn't want the job Ben had. We had been through hell and survived; we were very proud of what we had accomplished, and I was glad to have had the experience.

I couldn't wait to get home and see Lorrie and the kids. It was going to be a long flight from Bagram to Germany in the C-17, but it was worth it. The flight we were on turned out to be a medivac flight. There were four injured soldiers who were being evacuated to Germany. The injured soldiers were on stretchers and hooked up to monitors and IVs. It was a very solemn flight. We landed in Germany after a ten-hour flight. The next morning we boarded a commercial flight for the trip back to the United States.

We landed in Syracuse at 7:00 P.M., and there were Lorrie and the kids waiting for me. The kids ran up and jumped into my arms. I gave them and Lorrie a big hug. It was so good being back home—there had been times I didn't think I would ever see it again. We made our way through the airport and out to the parking lot. Lorrie handed me the keys so I could drive us home. As I was pulling out of the airport, I realized how strange it seemed driving a normal car on a real street. Lorrie had to remind me to turn the headlights on; we never drove with our headlights on in Afghanistan.

On the way home, I became very edgy, and I kept scanning the roadside. I was on the lookout for IEDs (Improvised Explosive

Devices). I knew there weren't any here, but it was a conditioned response. Physically I was in the United States, and I was safe, but in my mind I was still fighting the war. My brain was telling my body to get ready in case we were attacked. Lorrie knew I was different; I was having a hard time keeping up with a conversation, because I was so focused on the surroundings. She later told me she was surprised at how much my physical appearance had changed. My face now had that weathered look, and I had actually put on some weight from not being able to work out and eating the high-calorie MREs, plus all the cookies, cakes, and candy everyone sent me. We finally made it home; we spent the rest of the night catching up, and the kids showed me everything I had sent them. As I sat there listening to them, it seemed so surreal. Just a few days before, I was on a hilltop seven thousand miles away, being shot at. Now I was home.

It was two days before Christmas. Lorrie and I loved to decorate for Christmas. We had a tradition of decorating the house the weekend after Thanksgiving. We had three full-size trees that we put up along with all the other decorations. This year was much different. Lorrie had been struggling at home, and because we lived so far away from the unit, she didn't have the support that the other Syracuse wives had. Our oldest son, Seth, was having a hard time in school, and she was spending a lot of time meeting with his teachers. She was trying to be a mother and father to the boys along with dealing with all the problems that come with an old house. I didn't realize until I got home how much stress she was under.

That year, she went out and bought a live Christmas tree instead of trying to put the artificial ones together. She had put the tree up a couple weeks before. The dog kept drinking the water from the holder, the tree dried up, and all the needles were falling off. The kids hated the tree; they were afraid to walk by it, because they kept getting poked by the sharp needles. That first day back, we took the tree down and threw it out. I brought the artificial trees down from the attic, and we spent the day putting them up and decorating the house. It finally got us all in the Christmas spirit.

I only had ten days of leave, and they were going by fast. Everyone wanted to see me and spend time with me; it was really hard trying to find the time. My co-workers from school had a welcoming home party for me. I really enjoyed seeing them; they had all been so supportive. They wrote me letters, their classes sent me cards, and they did a large school supplies drive for the school we started in Lwara. After the party, we went to a hockey game. We loved going to hockey games, and that night one of my co-workers told the arena that I was home on leave from Afghanistan, and they announced it at the game. Christmas day, we had a large family gathering. Everyone wanted to hear what it was like, and I kept telling the stories over and over again. Even though I was home, I couldn't get away from the war.

The ten days home were the fastest ten days I had ever spent. It was hard to enjoy everything, because all I could think about was going back. This time, it was much different from when I first left. Then, I had no idea what it was going to be like, and we were excited about going. But this time, I knew exactly what I was in for, and that made it much harder. Plus, now I knew how hard it was on Lorrie while I was gone. There was nothing I could do to make it easier for her, and I hated that. It seemed like I had just got home, and now it was time to go back. The weather was terrible, and I was hoping that the flight would be cancelled so I could spend one more day with Lorrie and the kids—but it wasn't. This was one of the worst days of my life, having to tell them goodbye all over again, and this time it was much harder then it was the first time.

15

Orgun

Firebase Orgun was about the same size as Lwara; there were 150 soldiers stationed there. Just like in Lwara, the 82nd provided base security with a rifle platoon and mortar section. The 19th Special Forces Group had an A-team there along with the Civil Affairs team, and a Psychological Operations team as well. The base was about a mile southwest from the village of Orgun. Tim and Nino arrived at the base two weeks before; they weren't planning on taking any leave. Steve and I arrived at the base on January 5th. The weather had taken a drastic turn for the worse. There were about two inches of snow on the ground when we arrived.

Major Carlos Hernandez, the team leader for the CA team at Orgun, greeted us; he just recently had taken over the Orgun team. He was one of about ten soldiers from the 478th Civil Affairs Battalion from Miami, Florida, who mobilized with our October group. The original Orgun team leader had been reassigned to Bagram. The remaining members of the Orgun team were Sergeant First Class Jerry Woods, Staff Sergeant Paul Kelly, and Sergeant John Smith. Jerry and Paul were both police officers in Syracuse. John was a loan officer for a bank in Miami. Steve was real happy about going to Orgun. He worked with both of them in the police department, plus he was good friends with them off duty. I was also glad to be working with them, but I wasn't sure how it would work out with Carlos and me.

Carlos was a supervisor for the Dade County Public Works Department. He had a master's degree in Civil Engineering. His experience and education would come in handy as we prepared to build schools and wells. Jerry and Paul were glad we were coming to Orgun. They didn't know Carlos or John. I told them to be patient with him—he was their team leader. I knew Jerry and Paul would be looking to me for leadership, and I didn't want Carlos to think I was trying to run his team. I told my team that we would take a back seat for a while and let Carlos plan the missions. When I was in Bagram, Kellogg and I had talked about following up on some of the well proposals that I submitted in the Lwara Valley. My plan for our team was to eventually run separate CA missions to the east while the Orgun team concentrated on their own AO. We were going to have to work out the logistics for some overnight missions back to the Lwara Valley.

The 19th Special Forces Group A-Team commander at Orgun was Mitch Riley. The 19th Group was a National Guard Special Forces Unit from California. In the civilian world, Riley was a pharmaceutical salesman in Los Angles. He had a very calm demeanor—the complete opposite of Brady and Ross. Riley wanted his team to push out toward the east. He knew we were in Lwara, which was twenty miles east of Orgun. We had participated in a couple of patrols from Lwara to Orgun, so we were very familiar with the area. Steve and I met with Riley to fill him in on the AO. I told him that we submitted several projects in the Lwara valley, and our B-team wanted us to follow up on them. Riley told us that there had been a lot of Taliban activity in the valley since we pulled out. He had received an intelligence report that the Taliban did a full-scale attack on the AMF at firebase Lwara. The report said that the base was destroyed and several AMF soldiers killed. The report went on to say that aerial reconnaissance of the area showed what appeared to be Pakistan border guards operating a checkpoint next to the firebase. Riley wanted us to take a helicopter ride with him over the firebase to verify the report. I told him I wouldn't be surprised if they did move the checkpoint, because they tried to do it while we were there. Riley wanted to go the next day. Orgun was a FARP (Forward Arming and Refueling Point). There were always helicopters there, so it was easy to get a flight. A FARP is a temporary facility that provides fuel and ammunition for aircraft. FARPs are typically located in the main battle area, allowing aircraft to rapidly rearm and refuel.

It was a nice sunny morning. The past few days temperatures had been in the mid fifties, and all the snow had melted. Since the weather was good, Riley wanted to take the flight over Lwara. Riley and two of his team members, Sergeant Ron Hopper and Staff Sergeant Billy Mears, were going to accompany Steve and me on the flight. We would be flying in a Black Hawk helicopter with an Apache gunship escort.

We took off from Orgun at 10:00 A.M. Riley wanted to fly over some of the villages in the AO first so he could see their layout and the terrain leading in and out of the villages. We flew over Gayan first; it was about a five-minute flight from Orgun. I filled Riley in on Bakka Jan then pointed out his compound. There was a vehicle at his compound and five or six men around it. Riley wanted to circle around and get a better look. The men standing around the vehicle ran into the compound; they apparently didn't want us to know what they were doing. We then flew over Kaber Khel, Merbeck, and Arghamel. It was a different perspective flying over the villages. I could see a maze of trails that ran through the mountains. The insurgents used these trails to carry out attacks on us. Their use of the terrain and their knowledge of the trails made it very difficult to fight them. The mujahedeen used these same trails to fight and defeat the Russians.

A few minutes later, we were flying over Firebase Lwara. I couldn't believe what I saw. The firebase had been destroyed; bodies of dead AMF soldiers were scattered all around. The building we built for our hooch was completely leveled. The guard towers were destroyed and lay in a heap. I could see some people rummaging through the rubble. I just couldn't believe the destruction; it was obvious that whoever did this wanted to make a statement. As we circled around, we flew over one of the compounds close to the firebase. Steve spotted several rolls of concertina wire in the center of the compound. Riley pointed toward the east; about three hundred yards from the firebase, on the dry riverbed, were the Pakistan border guards. They had moved the checkpoint well into Afghanistan. I told the pilot to keep heading east, as I wanted to show Riley where the checkpoint should be.

As we were passing the ruins, a warning came on. The pilot looked to the right and said, "Hang on." We just had an RPG fired at us. He made a hard bank to the left, then a sharp dive. I was thrown against the side door, then it felt like I was coming down a steep roller coaster. I looked out the window and saw the white trail of the RPG go over us.

"Shit, they fired another one!" the pilot yelled.

"I see them; they are on a ridge to our right!" Riley said.

The pilot made another hard evasive maneuver, and now I felt like I was going to throw up. I really had a helpless feeling; there was absolutely nothing I could do but hold on. I didn't like to fly in the first place, and this wasn't helping matters. This time, the RPG went under us. I could hear the Apache pilot say he had a fix on the position. I turned and looked back toward the ridgeline in time to see the Apache fire two missiles at them. My heart was racing, and I was having a hard time catching my breath. We dodged another bullet; I wasn't sure how long our luck would last. Riley said he had seen enough, and we headed back to Orgun.

When we got back, we headed over to the OP center. We looked at the pictures I took of the firebase. Steve had taken some good pictures of the compound that had the concertina wire in it. It was shocking to see what happened to the base. As we looked through the pictures, I realized that the school was also gone. I wondered what happened to Mir Shir Khan.

"There's a lot going on in that valley," Riley said.

"The Taliban still has a strong hold on it," I replied.

"We need to get some operations going in that valley."

"We did, for six months; there is just too much support for the Taliban from the locals. They will take what you give them then turn around and shoot at you."

"We've got a lot of the same problems here. If we could knock out some of these warlords who are running the Taliban operations, things would be a lot better. The only reason they have support is the residents fear them."

"That's why they destroyed the firebase and killed the AMF. They wanted to send a message of what will happen to them if they support us."

"It's hard to win a battle like that. The Taliban knows we will eventually leave, and the locals know that too. That's why they are afraid to support us. I think once the Afghan National Army gets up and running, they will be the ones who will have to win that battle."

"What about the border guards?"

"I'll put it in the SITREP tonight about their incursion. Bagram can then deal with them."

After the flight, I really felt that the last four months had been a waste of time. The school we started was now gone, the firebase was destroyed, and several AMF soldiers had died. We did recover some weapon caches and had captured a member of Al-Qaeda. I didn't feel the outcome was worth it.

That night, we had our first rocket attack at Orgun. We were sitting in our tent playing cards when the air horn went off, signaling a rocket attack. The attacks here were nothing like in Lwara. We headed for the bunker and waited; nothing was happening. The rocket was fired from the mountain to the south and landed a long way away from the firebase. Paul told us that the firebase had never been hit by a rocket; they always landed short. Two Apaches took off and searched the area where the rocket was launched, but they didn't find anything. After about twenty minutes, the "all clear" sign was given, and we went back to playing cards.

The next couple of weeks, we spent assisting Hernandez's team with humanitarian aid distribution and visiting the villages in their AO. They had several well projects that had been submitted, and they had six wells that were being drilled. They also had a school being built in Orgun. Each day, we went to each project to check on the progress. They had an engineer from Bagram come to Orgun with plans for schools. The Army now wanted all schools to be built the same way, with specific building materials. They also had specifics on how the wells were to be drilled. When the engineer went back to Bagram, he left the plans with Hernandez. His background in engineering was a big help when it came to understanding the plans and making sure they were followed. They were very busy, but they didn't need two CA teams in Orgun. We became the security element for Hernandez's team. I really wanted to get out on our own. I called Bagram and talked with Kellogg. He said since they reorganized the teams, and the new teams that mobilized in November arrived, all the firebases had a CA team. We had to wait until something came up. Until then, we had to sit tight. Kellogg also told me that, due to the hostilities in the Lwara valley, all projects were on hold until further notice. I met with the team and told them it looked like we were staying put. They seemed to be fine with it.

The firebase at Orgun was far better than Lwara. The food was great; they had three hot meals a day. With Orgun being a FARP, there was a constant stream of supplies from Bagram. We had steaks, soft drinks, milk, cakes, and pies; there were no more MREs. They also had a satellite dish, and they got the Armed Forces network. There was a TV set up in the chow hall; we could watch CNN, ESPN, and all the networks. On January 27, 2003, at 2:30 A.M., we gathered in the mess hall and watched Super Bowl XXXVII. Things were going pretty well at Orgun. We also watched the United Nations hearings on Iraq. It looked like we were about to go to war there also. We all wondered, if we did go to war with Iraq, how that war would affect us. The biggest concern on everyone's mind was whether our replacements would show up or we would get stuck here longer.

Riley came to us. He had received information of a weapons cache in the village of Sarowbi. He said there were antiaircraft weapons and two Russian BTR-80s. The BTR-80 is an 8 × 8 Armored Russian Infantry fighting vehicle similar to the LAV-25 used by the Marine Corps. The village elder of Sarowbi is a former small-time warlord who was hiding the vehicles and weapons in his compound. Riley wasn't sure if the information was good or not. He wanted us to do a humanitarian mission to Sarowbi so he could get into the village and see if the information was true. Sarowbi was located about an hour southeast of Orgun.

We loaded our vehicles with cases of humanitarian meals. The plan was to go to the elders compound and give him the meals and let him distribute them. That way we could see if he did have anything. Our two CA teams, along with Riley's A-Team, went on the mission. Sarowbi was a small village with a population of about two hundred. Paul and Jerry had been here before, about two months ago, and proposed a well for the village. They met with the elder at that time, but they didn't get into his compound.

Hernandez's interpreter, Noor Walli, knew the elder very well. They were both former members of the mujahedeen and had fought the Russians here. Every time we went to a village or passed by a certain mountain, Noor had a story to tell us about a battle he had fought there. Noor knew the area very well, and he told us the elder probably did have the BTR, because he was with him when they captured them. Noor showed us where the elder's compound was. The elder came out and greeted Noor. They hugged each other, then Noor introduced us to him. We told him we had humanitarian meals for him to distribute to his residents. He was very happy and invited us in. He opened the doors to his compound so we could drive our vehicles in and unload them. As we pulled in, there sat the two BTRs. Riley went over to look at them, the elder came over and started telling him how he captured them from the Russians. He was very proud of them. They had been sitting there for nearly ten years. The tires were flat, and the batteries were dead. The antiaircraft gun sat in a corner all covered in rust.

Riley looked at us and laughed, "Well I guess the information was correct. I just never asked if they were operational. I guess he can keep his war relics."

The elder invited us to stay for chi; we sat there and listened to Noor and the elder tell us their war stories for the next hour. When the Russians moved into Orgun, Noor became a leader in the resistance movement. He rallied local men to fight the Russians. At the same time, the elder was leading the resistance movement in Sarowbi. Noor and the elder combined their forces and moved to the mountains. The Russians controlled the villages, but Noor and his fighters controlled the mountains. Noor and the elder would set up ambushes in the narrow passes. The Russians and their tanks were sitting ducks. The elder told us the Russians then began using their helicopters to attack the fighters in the mountains. This was very effective, and the fighters suffered heavy loses. Noor and his fighters fled to Pakistan.

It was there that he first met with American military advisors. He and his fighters were trained on the use of the Stinger missile system. The Stinger is a personal portable surface-to-air missile system that is light to carry and relatively easy to operate. Noor and the elder took their fighters, armed with the Stinger, back to the mountains surrounding Orgun to continue their fight against the Russians. When the Russians attempted to attack them with their helicopters, Noor used the Stinger to shoot them down. Noor and the elder were very proud of their victory against the Russians. They were also very appreciative for the help they received from the Americans, and that was why Noor was helping us now. Their stories were amazing; I couldn't imagine having to fight like this for the next twenty years the way they have. We thanked the elder for the chi and sharing his stories with us, and then we headed back to the firebase. The elder was allowed to keep his war trophies.

16

Operation Roll Tide

We received a message from Kellogg to pack up and get on the next flight to Bagram. We were being sent on a new mission. Kellogg didn't give us any details. I originally wanted our own mission, but now I was content. I really liked Orgun. If it was a new mission, I was sure we would be going someplace that didn't have the creature comforts that Orgun had. We arrived in Bagram the next day. It was February 12th. Kellogg told us the 20th Group had requested a CA team for an operation they would be conducting in the Madr and Kahmard Valleys of Bamiyan Province; it was called Operation Roll Tide.

The 20th Special Forces Group is headquartered in Birmingham Alabama; Operation Roll Tide was named after the University of Alabama's football team. Afghanistan was in the process of creating its own Army, and the United States was training those soldiers. The first 250 soldiers just finished their training, and the 20th Group was taking them on their first combat mission. The soldiers were organized into a battalion and designated as 1st Battalion ANA (Afghan National Army). Their mission was to find and destroy the warlord, Rahmatullah, and his army and stabilize the valleys. The mission would consist of just twelve Americans and the 250 Afghans. We were to be embedded with the Afghans and be their advisors on the mission. The 20th Group was sending ODB team 2030 (Operation Detachment Bravo). The Special Forces B-team is the headquarters element of a Special Forces Company; their mission is to establish and operate a firebase. Also going on the mission were three members of the 19th Special Forces Group ODA 952. They were the trainers who trained the Afghans, an Air Force Combat Controller, and our CA Team. An Air Force Combat Controller is a battlefield airman who is special operations trained and is a certified air traffic controller. Their mission is to deploy with Special Operational Forces into combat and hostile environments to conduct special reconnaissance while simultaneously conducting air traffic control, fire support, communications, and forward air control.

Bamiyan Province is northwest of Bagram. It was the site of the sixth-century Buddha statues that were carved into the side of a sandstone cliff. In 2001, the Taliban destroyed the statues, calling them idols, which were forbidden under Taliban law. Kellogg told us that we would be flying out that night around 10:00 P.M. The main force was already in place. They convoyed up there two days before. He said the mission would only last about two weeks, so we didn't need to take a lot of equipment. We did need to take a tent, so we went over to the bone yard and pieced together a GP small tent. The "bone yard" was the nickname given to an area where parts and pieces of all different types of equipment were stored. I figured that two weeks wasn't too bad. Kellogg said we would probably be sent back to Orgun at the completion of the mission.

We packed everything we thought we would need for two weeks. We were taking our Mercedes SUV, because they had a shortage of vehicles. At 10:00 P.M., we loaded up the Chinook and took off for Madr Valley. It was an eerie feeling flying at night. Madr Valley was located in the heart of the Hindu Kush Mountains. The helicopter was zigzagging around the mountains. It was a fifteen-minute flight from Bagram to Madr. Landing at this LZ was completely different from Lwara. The helicopter landed in the middle of a road. It was very dark, but I could tell we were surrounded by mountains. There wasn't the large security element waiting for us as there had been in Lwara. The security element consisted of two Americans and five Afghan soldiers. Major Matt Simpson, commander of ODB 2030, and Sergeant Major Tom Kelly greeted us. We loaded up our equipment and headed over to the firebase.

Matt Simpson was thirty-eight years old, slightly balding, and a little on the chubby side. He was the company commander for Bravo Company 2nd Battalion 20th Special Forces Group in Boston, Massachusetts. In the civilian world, he was a lawyer for a large Boston law firm. He was a graduate of Virginia Military Institute; he spent eight years on active duty, then left the Army and went back to college to study law. He decided that he wanted to get back into the Army on a part-time basis, so he joined the National Guard in 1998. Matt was single and accustomed to living the good life. He was always talking about the exotic sports cars he owned and his penthouse in Boston. Matt didn't want to share a tent with the rest of his team, so he had his own private tent. I thought Tim had a lot of movies until I saw his—he had more than five hundred DVDs. His tent was filled with all kinds of survival gear that he purchased just before he deployed. He said he hated the Army-issued equipment, which was why he bought his own. Matt spent most of his time planning missions, and he left the running of the base to his Sergeant Major Tom Kelly.

Sergeant Major Kelly was a tough, battled-hardened soldier with forty years in the Army, most of those spent in Special Forces. He was fifty-nine years old, just one year away from mandatory retirement. Because of his age, he wasn't supposed to deploy, but he requested a waiver, which the Army granted. He had done three combat tours in Viet Nam, all with the Special Forces. He was the prototypical, hard-nosed sergeant major. Everyone was afraid of him; he was quick to chew you out for the littlest infraction of his camp rules. No one wanted the wrath of the sergeant major to come down on him. He didn't care if you were a private or a major, he would let you know if you did something wrong. I tried not to cross his path, because I was a little intimidated by him. One night as we were waiting for a resupply, I struck up a conversation with the sergeant major. To my surprise, he was very talkative. He joined the Army in 1963, right out of high school. In 1965, he volunteered for Special Forces and did his first of three tours in Viet Nam in 1967. We talked about his experiences in Viet Nam, and he told me that the war we were fighting in Afghanistan was very much like the war he fought in Viet Nam. The enemy in Viet Nam was elusive, using hit-and-run tactics, and at night they would rocket their firebases just like in Afghanistan. In Viet Nam, he spent much of his time fighting the Viet Cong, an army that didn't wear uniforms and used guerilla warfare tactics, just like the insurgents in Afghanistan. The only difference, he said, was Viet Nam is a jungle, and Afghanistan is a desert.

We unloaded our gear and bunked in the supply tent that night. The next day, we were going to put our tent up, stow our gear, and meet with Simpson and our Afghan counterparts in the afternoon. That morning, we got up and went out to set up our tent. I was awestruck by our surroundings. The firebase was located in a saddle between these huge magnificent mountains. Looming up in the clear sky like giants, on the right there was one huge, solid wall with hardly an irregularity or break along the crest. The left mountain was strung along like a chain of agates; each seemed to be triangular with a switchback of paths that wound up and down the mountain.

The firebase was very small. The Afghans were set up on the western side with ten tents. The eastern side of the base was the American side. We had four tents and a generator. There were no shower facilities, and the only water we had was the bottled drinking water that we brought with us. We would not be able to get a shower until we got back from the mission.

We got our tent set up and our equipment stowed. The tent was just a four-man tent. We didn't have much room, but it was only going to last two weeks, and then we would head back to Orgun. I was a little concerned with the lack of protection that we had. There were no bunkers or fighting positions. There were no Hesco barriers as there were in Lwara and Orgun, just a barbwire fence surrounding the firebase. The only purpose the barbwire fence served was to keep the jackals out of the firebase. Jackals were similar to coyotes, and in this region of Afghanistan, they were very prevalent. If we came under attack like we did in Lwara, we wouldn't stand a chance.

That afternoon, we got together with Simpson, Kelly, Captain Brian Costly of ODA 972, and the commander of the ANA (Afghan National Army) Major Fahim Khan to discuss the operation. Costly was from Los Angeles, California, and a member of California National Guard's 19th Special Forces Group. He was thirty-five years old and tall, with an athletic build. In the civilian world, he was a police officer with the California Highway Patrol. The other two trainers with Costly, Sergeant First Class Andy West and Sergeant First Class Kevin Soto, were also police officers with the City of Los Angles Police Department. Steve and I immediately hit it off with them, and they were really glad to have us on board. I was glad we didn't have to prove ourselves to them.

Major Khan was from Kabul. He was forty-two years old and a Tajik. Tajik's are Sunni Muslims who originally came from Tajikistan. They make up the bulk of Afghanistan's educated elite. They are skilled artisans and traders. Many of them prosper enough to be considered middle class. Major Khan was married with four children—three boys and a girl. He was well educated, having graduated from Kabul University. He became a shopkeeper in Kabul, selling rugs. He eventually began to export his rugs to the West. He made a very good living and provided well for his family. When the Taliban took over, everything changed.

The Taliban instituted Sharia law, which decreed that the Afghan people would live a life like the Prophet Muhammad did fourteen hundred years ago. The law was interpreted to ban many activities. The Taliban outlawed movies, television, videos, music, dancing, hanging pictures in homes, clapping during sporting events, kite flying, alcohol, computers, statues, and beard trimming. Men were required to have a beard extending farther than a fist clamped at the base of their chin. Men were also required to keep their head hair short and wear a head covering. Women, in particular, were targets of the Taliban restrictions. Women were prohibited from wearing clothing regarded as stimulating and attractive. They were made to wear the burqa, a traditional dress covering the entire body except for a small screen to see out of. They were forbidden to ride in a taxi unless they had a close male relative with them. Employment for women was restricted to the medical field, because male medical personnel were not allowed to treat women. Women were not allowed to attend schools or participate in sporting activities. Households had to blacken their windows so women would not be visible from the outside. The Taliban had religious police patrolling the street enforcing the rules. If they caught someone violating the rules, they would beat them.

Major Khan's wife and daughter were not allowed to work in his store anymore. His wife and daughter would bring him his lunch every day, because now that they couldn't work in the shop, he couldn't leave. One day, as they left the shop, there was a strong wind blowing. The wind got under his daughter's burqa and blew it up past her knees. She immediately grabbed it and pulled it back down, but the religious police saw her legs, which was a violation. Two of them came over to her. They were armed with long sticks, and they began to beat her with them. Her mother begged them to stop, so they turned their attention on her and beat her with the sticks. Another shopkeeper who saw the beatings ran in and told Major Khan what was happening. He and the other shopkeeper ran out and convinced the religious police to stop beating them. He promised to take them home and not allow them out of the house anymore. He picked up his daughter and carried her home as his wife followed behind. His daughter suffered a broken arm, jaw, and nose; she was just fourteen years old. Major Khan said that all Tajiks were treated very badly by the Taliban.

He eventually had to close up his shop, because people were afraid of Taliban reprisals if they went inside. He took his family and fled north to Bazarak, in Panjshir Province. It was in Bazarak that Major Khan met up with his old friend from Kabul University, Ahmad Shah Massoud, the military leader of the United Islamic Front for the Salvation of Afghanistan—better known as the Northern Alliance. The Northern Alliance was made up of three different ethnic groups, the Tajiks, the Hazara, and the Uzbeks. They combined their forces into an alliance to fight the Taliban. Major Khan joined the Northern Alliance and quickly became one of Massoud's closest deputies. He was with Massoud on September 9th, 2001, when Massoud was assassinated by Al-Qaeda terrorists. Major Khan continued fighting with the Northern Alliance until December 2001, when the Northern Alliance gained control of Kabul. He and his family moved back to Kabul. He decided that he wanted to continue to help make Afghanistan a free and prosperous country as it had once been, so he joined the newly formed Afghanistan National Army.

Rahmatullah had his headquarters in the village of DoAbe, about an hour north of the firebase in the Kahmard Valley. Rahmatullah was a former Mujahedin leader during the Soviet War in Afghanistan. He was a member of the Hezb-e-Islami Gulbaddin, commonly referred to as the HIG. The HIG was founded in 1977 by Gulbaddin Hekmatyar. Hekmatyar opposed the 2001 American invasion of Afghanistan and allied himself with Mullah Omar, the Taliban leader, and Osama Bin Laden.

Rahmatullah was a loyal lieutenant of Hekmatyar. He was the commander of the HIG fighters operating in the Kahmard Valley. They were operating illegal checkpoints throughout the valley, charging locals a tariff to pass through. They threatened the locals with execution for anyone found helping American or Coalition forces. It was reported they had offered a bounty for anyone killing an American.

The mission was to kick off the next day at 7:00 A.M. We had to wait until daybreak, because the ANA didn't have night vision capabilities. We didn't have any close air support for the mission, because all air assets were being diverted to the Persian Gulf for the possible invasion of Iraq. Intelligence of DoAbe and Rahmatullah's headquarters was sketchy at best. We had some aerial photos of the area, but no one had been in the village to scout it out like we did in Gayan. We weren't exactly sure how many fighters Rahmatullah had. Some reports had the number at one hundred, but another said up to five hundred fighters. If we ran into a force of five hundred with no close air support, we were going to be in big trouble. Even if we ran into a force of one hundred who wanted to put up a fight, I didn't know what kind of determination the ANA soldier had. I was hoping they wouldn't be like the AMF soldiers, who were quick to turn around and run away from a fight. Costly said he had confidence in them; most of them had seen combat against the Russians, then fought the Taliban with the Northern Alliance.

There were two objectives: Rahmatullah's compound, which was located on the western edge of the village, and the government building, which he used as his headquarters located in the center of the village. DoAbe had a population of fifteen hundred people. There was a medical clinic and pharmacy in DoAbe. Dr. Mohd Ahfzal ran the clinic. Sixty to seventy patients were seen per day. Major Khan knew how important the clinic was to the residents, and I had him place it on a protected target list. He said he would make sure his soldiers protected it. The ANA battalion was organized into three companies of seventy-five soldiers each, plus a headquarters and mortar section consisting of twenty-five soldiers. Alpha Company was the attack force on the compound. Bravo would take the government building, and Charlie Company was a blocking force on the highway in and out of town. Major Khan and his headquarters element would operate out of the TOC (Tactical Operations Center) located a mile and a half south of the village. During the raid, Simpson would assist Khan in the TOC, Costly would go with Alpha Company, West with Bravo Company, and Soto with Charlie Company. Khan assigned four of his soldiers to secure the health clinic. Tim, Nino, Steve, and I would assist them.

The clinic was located on the northern edge of the village. The 1st and 2nd platoons of Charlie Company were securing the highway heading north out of town. We would follow them as they moved into position. As Alpha Company and Bravo Company began their assault on the compound and government building, we would move in and secure the clinic. Simpson, Costly, and Khan seemed satisfied with the plan; they had a lot of confidence in the ability of the ANA. I didn't have the same level of confidence that they had. The experience in Lwara taught me to always expect the unexpected. We didn't know how many fighters Rahmatullah had or what their capabilities were. The ANA were untested in battle, so we didn't know how they would perform. Steve had the same concerns. There was nothing we could do about it—just hope that Costly was right about the ANA and that everything went off according to the plan.

We were going to need an interpreter. Costly had four interpreters whom that he brought with him for the mission. He assigned Sultan Sultani to be our interpreter. Sultan was twenty-five years old. He was a Tajik and born in Kabul. His family fled Kabul during the Russian occupation. They moved to Iran, where Sultan and his six siblings grew up. Sultan attended the University of Tehran, where he studied engineering. He and his family moved back to Kabul after the Taliban withdrew. Sultan's older brother joined the ANA. Sultan wanted to serve also but, because of a birth defect to his right arm, he was unable to hold a gun. Sultan was fluent in English, so the recruiter offered him a job as an interpreter. Sultan was the complete opposite of Naime. He wore the ANA uniform and had no desire for blue jeans or any other Western wear. He didn't care anything about watching our movies, and he spent his off time with the other Afghans, whereas Naime wanted to spend all his off time with us.

Sultan took us around the ANA camp and introduced us to many of the soldiers. They were all busy cleaning their weapons and getting their gear ready for the mission. They all seemed very motivated and ready for the mission. I was glad that we spent some time with the ANA soldiers. Seeing their motivation made me feel better about the mission. They invited us to eat with them that night, and they served us rice with goat meat and Naan (Afghanistan bread). The ANA had their own cook, Abdul Rashul.

Abdul was forty-five years old, a Pashtun from Logar province south of Kabul. Abdul showed us his kitchen and demonstrated for us how he made the Naan. Naan-e-Afghani, which is commonly called Naan, is the national bread of Afghanistan. The bread is either oval or rectangular and is baked in a tandoor, a cylindrical oven that is the primary cooking equipment of the region. The tandoor sits above the ground and is made of bricks, which are heated to cook the bread. Abdul took his bread dough and stuck it to the interior wall of the tandoor to bake. He threw some black cumin seeds on it then scored lengthwise lines on it to add texture. It quickly puffs up and starts to color. It emitted a fresh bread smell that drew several of the ANA soldiers over to the kitchen area. Abdul then used two long iron tongs to pull the bread from the tandoor walls. The bread is very flat, with no firm crust. It has a dense and rich taste.

We sat on the ground with the ANA soldiers, and Abdul served us a large plate of rice with the goat meat on top. Each person was given a large piece of Naan. The plate of rice and goat was shared with six of us. Afghans use their hands to eat, thus the Naan acts as a fork and spoon. They tear the Naan into shreds then use the shreds to envelope the rice and goat meat so it can be picked up and conveyed to the mouth. As we sat there, we fumbled with the bread and rice, dropping most of the rice before we got it to our mouths. The ANA soldiers laughed, then they showed us how to hold it in our fingers and pack the rice in the bread. A little practice, and they had us eating like we were one of them.

We left the firebase at 7:00 A.M. the next day for DoAbe. The ANA led the way, and we positioned ourselves in the middle of the convoy right behind Major Khan's vehicle. The route to DoAbe took us through several mountain passes. The views were spectacular. The huge snow- capped mountains seemed to engulf us. Several of the mountains were full of caves. Sultan told us the Russians would kill the residents of an entire village then hide the bodies in a cave. Then, during the Taliban reign, the locals would hide possessions outlawed by the Taliban in the caves.

We made our way to the release point, about a mile and a half south of the village. Major Khan set up his TOC, and the mortar section set up their 60-mm mortar tubes. At 8:30 A.M., the attack teams left the release point and moved to their staging areas just outside the village. We followed Sergeant Mohd Anwar's platoon. Sergeant Major Kelly was accompanying him. The platoons quickly moved in and secured the road heading north out of the village. The clinic was about a quarter mile to the east of our position. As soon as the road was secured, we made our way to the clinic. The assault was to commence at 9:00 A.M.; we needed to secure the clinic before the start of the assault.

Corporal Safieullah was in charge of securing the clinic. He had three other soldiers with him. As soon as we got to the clinic, they immediately set up a perimeter. Tim and Nino assisted them. Safieullah, Sultan, Steve, and I entered the clinic. Dr. Mohd Ahfzal was there, along with his helper and pharmacist Mohd Daud. Safieullah introduced himself and told Dr. Ahfzal he was with the Afghan National Army, and they were there to arrest Rahmatullah and his soldiers. Sultan introduced us and told the doctor we were Americans assisting the Afghan National Army in ridding Afghanistan of the Taliban and warlords like Rahmatullah, and that we were going to protect his clinic during the arrest. The doctor gave us all a hug and told us, "Thank you." He said Rahmatullah was evil, and he was so glad to get rid of him. He offered us tea; I told him we couldn't then but would when we were done with the mission. Safieullah told the doctor and his helper to stay inside until the operation was over; he would tell them when it was safe.

We went back outside and took up a position; it was 8:55 A.M. A couple of minutes later, I heard an explosion and some gunfire coming from the compound, then everything went eerily quiet. Soto came on the radio and said the government building was secure. A few minutes later, Costly came on and said the compound was secure. I couldn't believe it—the operation was over in fifteen minutes, and there were no casualties. As it turned out, Rahmatullah got word of the operation and fled the area along with his fighters. He was later captured in the province of Oruzgan. At the time of his capture, Rahmatullah was in possession of anthrax powder and a liquid poison that he planned to distribute to Al-Qaeda and Taliban operatives in preparation for future attacks on Untied States and Coalition forces. The poison attacks were to target water sources, to include reservoirs. He was sent to Guantanamo Bay detention facility in Cuba. On April 30, 2008, Rahmatullah was repatriated along with eight other detainees. Rahmatullah joined the Taliban in Pakistan in February 2009 and is now a senior Taliban leader.

The gunfire that I heard turned out to be one of the ANA soldiers shooting a dog that attacked him. There was no one at the compound but they did find a huge weapons cache. At the government building was Dur Mohd, Rahmatullah's assistant. He was very cooperative; he gave us the locations where we could find three more weapon caches and where Rahmatullah was headed.

We spent the rest of the day loading up the weapons cache and assessing the needs of the village. We had tea with the doctor; he told us he needed more beds for his patients, vaccines, IV solutions, and various types of medicines. We told him we had a lot of the medicines he needed back at our firebase and we would give him what he needed. We also visited DoAbe's school. The temporary school building was located in a warehouse in the center of town. They currently had approximately two hundred boys and girls in grades one through six. Mohd Rahim was the headmaster of the school, and he said he had ten teachers. They were in need of a new building. The original school building was destroyed during the fighting between the Northern Alliance and Taliban. They were also in need of school supplies. I told him we would submit a proposal for a new school.

We made it back to the firebase and sent off our SITREP. It was a good day, although many of the ANA soldiers were disappointed that they didn't get into a fight. I was glad we didn't, and so were Steve, Tim, and Nino. We had seen enough fighting in Lwara, and Nino had seen a lot in Asadabad.

17

Firebase Romero

Operation Roll Tide was a success. Rahmatullah fled the valley and was on the run. We were anxious to pack up and get back to Orgun. It looked like we were going to convoy back; flights were very limited now because of the buildup in the Persian Gulf. We started packing everything up; we were going to leave the next morning, and it would be a three-day drive back to Bagram. Simpson came over to our tent and told us to stop packing. He had just gotten the word from Bagram that Lieutenant General Dan McNeill, commander of military operations in Afghanistan, that President Hamid Karzai had decided to create a permanent firebase in the Madr Valley. They want the ANA to establish themselves as the legitimate military organization and to disarm the Madr and Kahmard Valleys. President Karzai wanted an assessment of the needs of the villages in the valleys, and he would personally make sure the needs were addressed. I just had a feeling that something like this was going to happen because we didn't bring much of our gear with us. Simpson said that Bagram was loading up four large Kamaz trucks full of supplies for us, and they should be here in three or four days. One of the trucks has been dedicated for us, and our B-team was loading all of our equipment.

We were going to miss Orgun's nice amenities, but we were happy to have our own mission. Simpson said that within the next few weeks, Bagram was going to send out a team of engineers to build us latrines and a shower facility. I got on the satellite phone and called

Kellogg back in Bagram. He told me this was becoming a real high priority. Karzai wanted to show the people that the ANA will protect them from the warlords and thieves, and that he was serious about rebuilding Afghanistan. He wanted to use our mission as a model. Then, as other battalions of the ANA graduatee from their training, they would move into other provinces and secure them.

He told me to be prepared for a lot of high-ranking visitors. General McNeill was planning on visiting the firebase in the near future, and I would have to brief him on our operations. That was just great; I didn't like briefing colonels, let alone a three-star general. Kellogg said he was making sure we got all of our equipment. I was concerned about the safety of the equipment, but he said the trucks were going to have a military escort. Kellogg also told me that there were four members from the 412th Civil Affairs and that the unit that will be replacing us was meeting with him in Bagram. They were planning the handoff; their unit would be here in May, and we should be back home by the first of June. That was great news—there was finally a light at the end of the tunnel. With the war looming in Iraq, we didn't know if we would get stuck here longer, but then we knew who is replacing us and when. We had a lot of work to keep us busy until then, so we expected time to go by fast.

We got together with Simpson, Costly, and Major Khan to plan some missions and set some priorities. There were six villages in Madr Valley and twenty villages in the Kahmard Valley. We decided to concentrate on the villages in the Madr Valley first, then push out to the villages in the Kahmard Valley. The villages in the Madr Valley were all within a thirty-minute drive from the firebase. The villages in the Kahmard Valley were all at least an hour away, and some were a two-hour drive. To get to the Kahmard Valley, we had to go through some narrow mountain passes. The weather was going to dictate what we could do. It was now the middle of February, and one day the temperature would be sixty degrees, then the next day we would get ten inches of snow. The weather in the mountains was highly unpredictable. The six villages in Madr Valley were Madr, Paghmania, Ta Tara, Zair Som, Do Sakh, and Do Ru. We were going to visit each of the villages, meet with the elders, and assess their needs. Major Khan was going to explain to the elders that the ANA was now the legitimate military organization of the new democratic government of Afghanistan, and their job was to disarm the valley and provide security and stability there.

Simpson said we needed to name our firebase. In the beginning firebases were named after the closest village like Lwara and Orgun, but now they were changing the names to the name of a soldier that was killed in action in Afghanistan. Costly said he would like to name it Firebase Romero in memory of Sergeant First Class Daniel Romero, a member of Bravo Company 5th Battalion 19th Special Forces Group who was killed in action on April 15th, 2002, in Kandahar, Afghanistan. We all thought that was a great idea, and the firebase then became Firebase Romero.

Our first mission was to the village of Madr. It was a fifteen-minute drive along a rutted dirt road in a canyon hedged by razor sharp cliffs. The village of Madr had a population of approximately four thousand people of Tajik ethnicity. As soon as we entered the village, Major Khan deployed his soldiers in defensive positions throughout the village. Village Elder, Hajji Abdul Satr, greeted us and welcomed us to his village. He invited us into his residence for tea and bread. Major Khan and two of his soldiers, along with Steve, Tim, Nino, Sultan, and me, joined Elder Hajji Abdul Satr and eight of his friends for tea. We sat in a circle on the floor in his reception room because he had no furniture. It was dark and musty smelling; there was a picture of Massoud on the wall. Major Khan started out telling the elder how the ANA was now the legitimate army of Afghanistan, and they were here to secure the valley and assist the villages with whatever needs they had. Major Khan introduced us and explained how America was helping to rid the country of the Taliban and assisting the Afghan government with rebuilding the country. The elder was very happy that we were here. Major Khan also told the elder that if they had any weapons, they needed to turn them over to the ANA. The elder told us that they were tired of fighting, and we could have all of their weapons. This was definitely a different reception from what we got in Lwara.

The elder then motioned to one of his sons; he brought in a pitcher of water and a basin. He went around and set the basin in front of us then poured the water over our hands. I knew they got the water from the stream that ran along side the village, because the water was brown. Then another son brought a towel for everybody to dry their hands on. It was obvious this towel had never been washed, and by the time it got to me, ten other people had already dried their hands on it. My hands were now dirtier than they were before they poured the muddy water over them. Steve was sitting next to me, and he leaned over to me and said, "My hands are now all gritty, and that water really smelled bad."

"I know, my hands smell really bad," I replied.

"Great, I don't have any hand sanitizer, do you?"

"No, Tim do you have any hand sanitizer?"

"No, I wish I did. That water was terrible. Nino, you got any?"

"Look what I got! You know I'd take care of you."

We all used the hand sanitizer, but we did it discreetly. The elder's one son brought around the Naan and gave everybody a piece. Then the other son brought out several plates of eggs over easy. Everybody broke off a piece of bread and dipped it into the eggs. It was really difficult sitting on the floor with our body armor and cargo vests on while trying to lean forward to dip the bread in the eggs. Then one of the sons brought everyone out a cup, and the other son brought out what I thought were pitchers of lemonade. I was really surprised that they had lemonade, I had never seen it before. I leaned over and asked Sultan if in fact it was lemonade, because he was drinking a glass of it. Sultan told me no, it was just water. The water was so murky, I had thought it was lemonade. They just scooped the water out of the creek. Major Khan and his soldiers were drinking it along with the elder and his friends. I told Sultan to apologize to the elder for us and explain to him that we can't drink the water—we're not used to it, and we could become very sick. The elder nodded and smiled. He motioned to his sons, and they brought us out tea. I knew they made the tea with the same water, but they boiled it, so we should be all right.

When we finished eating and drinking, the elder took us on a tour of the village and pointed out things they needed. His first major concern was the condition of their road. It was in poor shape and washed out numerous times throughout the rainy season. Having just traveled on it from the firebase to Madr, I could attest to the poor condition. He would like to have it rebuilt from Madr to the border of Samagan, a distance of approximately twenty miles. There were no water wells in the village. The only supply of water came from the nearby stream. He would like the installation of a well and water reservoir for farm field irrigation and storage. The stream flows year round; the elder said he would like a motor that could be utilized by the stream flow to generate electricity for the village. He also requested staple items such as wheat, corn, and rice.

We then walked over to the school; he was very proud of it. They had 450 male students and 250 female students in grades one through six, but they were short on school supplies. We told the elder that we could help supply many of the things he needed. We could give him a well, the staple items, and school supplies. We would put in a request for the roadwork and generator. He was very appreciative. He then walked us over to a warehouse in the center of the village. He opened the door, and inside was a huge weapons cache. There were mines, mortars, mortar tubes, rocket propelled grenades and launchers, cases and cases of ammunition, and at least 250 AK-47s. He told us to take it—they were done fighting, and they just wanted to live in peace now. Major Khan thanked the elder for his cooperation then invited him to the firebase next week for a Jurga we would be holding. The elder shook our hand and told us he was looking forward to working with us. Major Khan motioned to his soldiers to load up the weapons cache, and we headed back to the firebase. I was really pleased with how well our meeting went in Madr. This was so much different from Lwara; I felt we could really make a difference here.

The next day, we traveled to the village of Zaire Som and met with Abdul Bagui, the village elder. The village had a population of five hundred people of Tajik ethnicity. Bagui was much younger than most elders; he was in his early to mid thirties. He was short, with a big round belly. He reminded me of a used car salesman; he was always smiling, and he kept patting us on the back. Major Khan explained why we were here just like he did in Madr; and just like in Madr, the elder invited us to eat with him. Of course, Major Khan couldn't pass up a free meal, plus we would have offended him if we didn't stay after he invited us.

We gathered in the elder's reception room just like we did in Madr. Abdul Bagui had invited some other members of the village to join us. His room was a little nicer than Elder Satr of Madr. Bagui had some very nice rugs on the floor and pillows along the walls to lean on. The process was just the same as it was in Madr; Bagui had his sons waiting on us. He motioned to them, and they brought a basin and pitcher of water and went around to everybody and poured the water over our hands, then sent one towel around for everyone to dry their hands. Steve, Tim, Nino, and I all reached into our pockets and pulled out our hand sanitizer—we were prepared this time. The same creek that ran past Madr ran past Zair Som; the water was still dirty and smelly. Bagui served us rice with goat meat, Naan, and tea. I was sitting next to one of the village members on one side and Sultan on the other. Across from me were Bagui and Major Khan. The four of us shared a plate of rice and goat meat. Then, as a special treat, Bagui served us freshly made yogurt. His son brought out a big bowl of it with a spoon. Everyone took turns with the spoon, scooping up a big spoonful of the yogurt. The yogurt was warm and very bitter. Sultan leaned over to me and said this was the best yogurt he had ever had. I told Sultan he didn't know what good yogurt was.

We finished our meal, and Bagui took us on a tour of the village. His village had many of the same needs as Madr. The road was in bad condition, and they were in need of a water well. Bagui expressed a desire to have a pedestrian bridge constructed over the creek that flows through the middle of the village. He said that, during the spring thaw, the creek becomes so high it can be very hazardous to cross. Major Khan told Bagui that we could help him with many of the projects, but they needed to turn over any weapons that they had. Bagui said he had a small weapons cache that he would be glad to turn over. Khan had his soldiers load up the weapons, and we thanked him for the meal and told him we would be in touch.

We finished the week off by visiting the Paghmania, Do Ru, Do Sakh, and Ta Tara. Their needs were basically the same as Madr and Zair Som. Everyone was very welcoming and friendly toward us. During the reign of the Taliban, the Tajiks were treated very badly. They were glad that Afghanistan now had a democratic government and the Afghanistan National Army to protect them. They were all very willing to turn their weapons over to us. We invited all the elders to a Jurga that we were going to hold at the firebase in two weeks. They were all looking forward to the Jurga and working with us.

A few days later, the convoy with our supplies arrived along with a team of four engineers. They built latrines and a shower stall, they set up Hesco barriers around the camp, and they brought a new generator that gave us power for the whole base. They left us several sheets of plywood, two by fours, and nails. Our B-Team sent us all of our equipment, including a Yukon stove. Our tent filled up with all of our gear and stove, and it became very cramped, but at least we were warm, and we had our movies.

The next week, we visited several villages in the Kahmard Valley. We assessed the needs of those villages just like we had with the villages in Madr Valley. One day we were going to visit the village of Roy Sang. It was a good two-hour drive from the firebase. The village of Laghaki was halfway between the firebase and Roy Sang. We were going to stop there on our way to Roy Sang. Afghanistan is located in a geologically active part of the world. The Hindu Kush mountain range is hit by dozens of earthquakes each year.

Afghan homes are made of dried mud, so even moderate earthquakes can cause many deaths and major damage to infrastructure.

Many of the villages in the Kahmard Valley were located at the base of a mountain next to the river that cut through the valley. The villagers used these rivers for their source of water. Laghaki sat right at the bottom of a mountain. We followed a winding road that ran parallel to the river. As we got close to Laghaki, the road became littered with rocks that had tumbled off the mountain. As we rounded a corner, we were shocked by what we saw. There had been a massive landslide due to an earthquake, and the village of Laghaki was completely destroyed. Most of the buildings had been crushed by massive boulders, and the buildings that weren't crushed by the boulders had collapsed during the shaking. We searched for survivors but found none. Four days before, I was in the operations center talking with Kellogg and Costly when the building began to shake. We ran outside, for fear of the building collapsing. The ground shook, and I could hear a rumbling through the valley; it lasted about thirty seconds. I knew right away that it was an earthquake, even though I had never experienced one before. Costly had been through a couple before in California, but he had never felt one that strong. It was this earthquake that had destroyed Laghaki. I couldn't help think how hard life was for the Afghan people. They have lived through decades of war and persecution, they didn't have any of the basic necessities such as running water, electricity, and health care that we take for granted in America, and they constantly live with the threat of a natural disaster.

We continued on to Roy Sang, where we met with the village elder, Gulan Sakhy. The village had a small health clinic run by a husband-and-wife doctor team. Several survivors of Laghaki made it to Roy Sang and were treated in the clinic. Dr. Faizulla told us he was in need of bandages and splints. There were fifteen displaced families from Laghaki staying in Roy Sang. We told the doctor that we could help him out with those supplies and that we would be requesting assistance from Bagram for the displaced families. We invited Elder Sakhy to the Jurga that we were hosting the next week, and he told us he would be there. On our SITREP that night, I informed Bagram of the situation at Laghaki and requested any assistance they could provide. I received a message back that they would be sending a med cap out in the next couple of weeks. They also said that an NGO organization from Kabul was sending a team out to assist with the displaced citizens in Roy Sang.

It got very cold at night, and we were really glad to have the Yukon stove. The stove burned diesel fuel. It was slow burning, and the fumes were not explosive like gasoline fumes. We had a five-gallon can of diesel fuel outside the tent, with a hose running from the container to the stove. A five-gallon can lasted about seven hours. We would turn the stove on about 7:00 P.M. Then, at 2:00 A.M., we would have to switch out the empty can with a full can. It was Nino's responsibility to get up at 2:00 A.M. and switch out the cans. Nino had a spare ready to go, because he didn't want to walk all the way across the firebase in the freezing cold at 2:00 A.M. to fill up a can. One night Nino went out to switch the cans, and the spare can was empty. Someone switched our full can for their empty can. The next night, the same thing happened. The third night, Nino filled the spare can with gasoline instead of diesel. It was about 1:00 A.M., and there was a large boom in the tent next to us. As soon as the gasoline hit their stove, it blew the top off their stove and filled their tent with smoke. Then we knew who was taking our fuel. They never said anything to us, and we never said anything to them, but they never took our spare can of fuel again.

It was now March, the snow had melted, and about three days a week it would rain. We were now living in a mud bowl. The dry riverbeds and small creeks had become raging rivers. It was nearly impossible to get around. Some days, we couldn't leave the firebase because of the mud—our vehicles just wouldn't go. It became very difficult just to walk around the base. The mud was nearly ankle deep at times. We were constantly scraping the caked on mud off our boots. Many of the villages in the valley were accessible only by foot. We would leave a security detail with the vehicles then traverse small winding trails leading into to a village. We would slip and slide on the mud, falling down five or six times before we reached the village. By the time we got back to the firebase, we were covered in mud. We spent hours scraping the mud off our equipment.

Simpson had hired six locals to work at the firebase like we had done in Lwara. The workers were busy filling the Hesco barriers and making repairs to the Op center. All of our uniforms were a mess; it had been over a month and a half since we were able to wash our clothes. I had Sultan find one of the locals who was interested in doing our laundry. Sultan found Abdul Ahmed, a thirty-four-year-old Tajik from Ta Tara (a small village just a couple of miles south of the firebase). I told Abdul I would pay him an additional twenty dollars a week for doing our laundry. I knew Abdul wouldn't do the laundry himself but would have his wife do it. Just like in Lwara, Abdul would take the laundry home, and his wife and daughters would take it to the river and wash it. We always saw women perched along a riverbank washing clothes; they would then spread them out on the rocks to dry.

Abdul was very excited to get the extra job, and he kept thanking us for it. I had Sultan explain to him that we wrote our first name on our laundry bag and on our clothes and to make sure he put the same clothes back in the laundry bag that he took the clothes out of. I knew that I was wasting my time telling him that, because in Lwara we never got the right clothes back. We always spent part of a day going from tent to tent finding our clothes, but since this was a small base, maybe that would work out better. Abdul said he would pick the clothes up on Tuesday and have them back to us on Thursday. I thought that was a pretty fast turnaround. In Lwara, it took five days before we got them back, but I again attributed it to being a smaller number.

That first Tuesday came, and Abdul had thirteen laundry bags to take home. He brought two of his sons with him to help carry the bags. We couldn't wait to finally get some clean clothes. Thursday afternoon came and, just like Abdul said he would, he brought back all thirteen bags. I gave him his money and thanked him, and he in turn thanked me for the opportunity. It was really funny how everyone was so excited about finally getting clean laundry. It had been the topic of conversation around the firebase for the past two days. It was like Christmas: we were all eagerly waiting for Santa Claus to bring us our presents.

We grabbed our laundry bags and ran back to our tents to change into our clean clothes. We ripped open our bags and pulled our clothes out, just like kids opening their Christmas presents. As soon as I pulled the clothes out, I couldn't believe the stench that was coming from our clothes. Now I knew how Abdul got our clothes back to us so fast. His wife dried our clothes over a campfire. Now all of our underwear, socks, and uniforms smelled like burned wood. She must have held them directly over the smoke to dry them. I thought our tent smelled bad before, but this was terrible. We all looked at each other in disbelief. It was just a matter of minutes, and everyone was standing outside his tent, holding the laundry bags. I knew Abdul didn't intentionally try to ruin our laundry—he was so proud when he handed it back to us. He thought he was helping us out by getting it back so fast.

The next morning, Sultan and I sat down with Abdul. I thanked him for doing our laundry, but told him we couldn't have him dry it over a fire, because it made the clothes smell bad. He was very apologetic and said he would take them right then and fix them. He was worried that he would lose the job. I told him not to worry, it was just a mistake. He didn't have to get our clothes back to us so fast; it was all right to let them air dry. After that first try, we never had another problem with our laundry and, unlike with Lwara, we always got back our own clothes.

It had been three weeks since our last resupply, and we were running low on MREs and bottled water. A couple of weeks before, I got a call from Kellogg. He told me that it would be awhile before our next resupply, the Army was gearing up for war with Iraq, and most of the air assets were being diverted to that theater of operations; we needed to make do with what we had.

On our last resupply, our B-team sent us a satellite radio, and we were able to pick up CNN. The days we couldn't leave the firebase, we would sit and listen to the war coverage in Iraq. I found it so ironic; here I was fighting one war and listening to another war on the radio. It reminded me of the time I sat in front of the television watching CNN broadcast the Persian Gulf War and wishing I could be part of it. Now, thirteen years later, I'm again listening to CNN broadcast another war, but this time my feelings are completely opposite. I wished I were home watching it on my television.

I really couldn't understand why President Bush wanted to go to Iraq. Al-Qaeda and the Taliban still had a strong hold on southeastern Afghanistan and the tribal area of Pakistan. Osama Bin Laden and Mullah Omar were still on the run. What we needed were more troops and resources, but instead we were losing what few resources we had to fight another war. We were getting critically low on supplies. We had only one case of bottled water left, we were all out of MREs, and our medical supplies were getting low. Simpson called in an emergency resupply. We were told that the Air Force was going to do an air drop of supplies and mail to us. The plane would be coming out of Uzbekistan, and the drop would be a night-time drop at 11:30 P.M., in two days. We couldn't believe that they had to send a plane from Uzbekistan, but at this point we didn't care where it came from—we just needed our supplies.

Staff Sergeant Tommy Crowe was our Air Force Combat Controller. He was twenty-eight years old and an Air Force reservist from Seattle, Washington. Tommy was a little concerned with the idea of doing an air drop on our location. We didn't have a big LZ like we had in Lwara. There was a small field adjacent to the firebase, and the crew on the resupply mission would have to be precise on the drop or we would be hunting the mountaintops for our supplies. The plane was to fly over and drop our supplies by parachute. Tommy marked the LZ with infrared strobe lights. The plane was to come from the north and fly on a southerly heading following the valley, then make the drop over the LZ. It was an hour flight from Uzbekistan to our firebase.

We set up our security; the ANA assisted us with it. We were all in place by 11:00 P.M., and then we waited. At 12:30 A.M., we were still waiting. Tommy finally got the word that the plane was running late. They had just left Uzbekistan, and the drop wouldn't happen until 1:30 A.M. Finally, at 1:45 A.M., Tommy made radio contact with the plane, and they were ten minutes out. We started scanning the sky with our night vision goggles and listened for the roar of the engines. The supplies would be placed on pallets and attached to parachutes. The pallets would have IR strobes on them, too, so we could see them. It was a very dark and overcast night, which made the mission even more difficult.

Off in the distance, we could hear the plane; they were looking for the LZ. Tommy made radio contact with them and was trying to walk them in. We could hear the plane coming from the west and not the north. We finally made a visual contact with the plane. It was about four miles off to our west. Then, to our disbelief, they made the drop, but they had completely missed the LZ. I counted six parachutes drifting off into the dark, and all of our supplies and mail were scattered across the Hindu Kush Mountains. Costly was with the ANA on top of a ridge west of the firebase. He radioed that he thought he had a fix on the location of the drop. It looked like the parachutes came down in the vicinity of Do Sakh. Tommy said they had dropped eight pallets of supplies.

Everyone immediately took off for Do Sakh. One of the problems we faced was that when the Russians were here, they heavily mined the valley, and many areas still hadn't been cleared of the mines yet. It was going to be very dangerous walking around at night looking for our supplies. Costly and his ANA team made it to Do Sakh first. He radioed that he found a parachute and one of the pallets. We all responded to Do Sakh and began the search for our supplies. The water pallet landed in the center of the village and broke apart upon impact; there were hundreds and hundreds of water bottles scattered all over. We spent the next four hours recovering our supplies. We found letters and packages from home scattered all over. It looked like the mail pallet came apart in the air, because the mail was scattered over such a large area. We recovered nine of the ten pallets that were dropped. Fortunately, no one was injured during the recovery. What upset us the most was losing our mail. We recovered only a portion of what was sent to us. Not only did we miss out on homemade cookies and cakes, but whoever found it would now have our names and home addresses. We could only hope that the mail ended up in the river that ran next to the village.

We got word from Bagram that the Med Cap would be here the first week in April. There were two doctors coming, and one was a female. Male doctors could not treat women. Many times, we would have men come to the firebase and ask for medicine for their wives and daughters. Our medic would ask them to bring them in so he could see what was wrong, but the Afghan men wouldn't allow our medic to see their wives or daughters. Two veterinarians were coming also. At our Jurga meeting, all of the elders asked for help for their animals. Many of their horses, donkeys, and goats were sick and needed care. When the medical team arrived, we set up two tents for treatment. one for males and one for females. We also set a special area just outside the firebase for animals. We ran the Med Cap for three days—twelve hours a day. They treated more than eight hundred people, nearly half women. The veterinarians treated three hundred animals. A reporter from one of the news organization accompanied the Med Cap and wrote an article on the success of the Med Cap and how the ANA had disarmed the valley and brought peace to this part of Afghanistan.

I flew back to Bagram with the Med Cap team to see the dentist. I had lost a filling two months ago, and my tooth was really bothering me. Bagram had really changed since we first arrived in September. They had built a big PX (Post Exchange), big dining facilities, and a big gym. I took my old tattered uniforms and traded them in for some new ones. All the tents now had a wooden structure with separate sleeping quarters. They all had air conditioning and television. Each camp at Bagram had a shower facility with running water. Each camp also had an Internet café with twenty computers; I was able to use email again. I talked with Lorrie every day on line. The VFW had sent thousands of phone cards to Bagram, allowing soldiers to make free phone calls home. I was able to use the phone every night to call home and talk with Lorrie and the kids.

By the middle of April, the rain was over, the mud had dried up, and the raging rivers were now bubbling creeks. The valleys were covered with a lush green carpet of grass. I had just returned from

Bagram. Simpson told me they got the word that the 20th Group's tour of duty was up, and they were pulling out the following week. They were being replaced by the 3rd Special Forces Group.

There was still one village in the eastern Kahmard Valley that we hadn't visited yet, and that was the village of Chokordara. It was a three-hour drive from the firebase, but Simpson wanted an assessment done so he could give a full briefing of all the villages in the AO to his replacement. We didn't know anything about the village, and neither did Major Kahn.

On our way there, I was driving one of the four-door Toyota Hilux pickup trucks. The driver side of the Hilux was on the right side, Sultan was riding in the left front passenger seat, and Simpson and Nino were in the back seats. We were about halfway to Chokordara when we rounded a corner in the valley and came across acres and acres of poppy plants. Sultan told me that these poppy fields belonged to Rahmatullah and that was how he financed his army. The Afghans derive opium from the poppy plant, which is later refined into heroin. Opium production accounts for sixty percent of Afghanistan's economy.

We were about a mile from Chokordara when we came to a narrow earthen bridge that crossed a steep ravine. We got out and surveyed the bridge. We determined that it would never hold the Humvees or the ANA's Kamaz, but we figured it would hold the Mercedes and the Hilux. Steve was driving the Mercedes, and he drove across the bridge with no problem. Major Khan had three vehicles similar in size to the Mercedes, and they went across with no problem. The soldiers riding in the Kamaz and Humvee walked across the bridge. They were going to hop into the back of the Hilux and Major Khan's vehicles. Mine was the last vehicle to cross the bridge.

I was almost across when the bridge on my side started to give way. My right front tire slipped off the bridge, and the vehicle began to roll over. The left rear tire was about three feet up in the air, and I was looking straight down the ravine. The vehicle stopped sliding and was now teetering on the bridge. Sultan and Simpson bailed out when that happened, and the vehicle shifted more. My right front tire was completely off the bridge now, and the front of the vehicle kept sliding farther off the bridge. Nino jumped out and grabbed hold of the vehicle. Several ANA soldiers ran over and grabbed hold to try to stop it from sliding off. I was trying to get out, but it was very difficult. The cab was very small, my equipment kept catching on everything, and I had to climb nearly straight up to get out the passenger door. Just then, Nino jumped up on the side of the vehicle and reached down inside, grabbed a hold of my cargo vest, and pulled me out of the vehicle. Just as I got out, more of the bridge gave way and the Hilux dropped down the fifty-foot ravine.

I lay on the ground, my heart pounding, and it took me a couple of minutes to regain my composure. I looked at Nino and said, "I knew there was a reason that I agreed to take you on our team."

We laughed and Nino said, "Now you owe me."

"I sure do!"

"That's too close of a call for a short timer," Simpson said.

Major Khan sent a couple of his soldiers down the ravine to retrieve our equipment in the Hilux. The village elder of Chokordara Abdul Raouf heard we were coming to visit him but were having a problem at the bridge. He brought several of his residents to greet us and fix the bridge. He apologized for our mishap but said they were desperately in need of a new bridge. I told him I could attest to that. He invited us to his residence for tea. The rest of the men he brought with him repaired the bridge.

We sat and had tea with him. There were about five hundred residents in his village, all of Tajik ethnicity. Chokordara was just like all of the other villages in the valley, in need of a water well, road work, electricity, and medicine. We told Elder Raouf that we would be submitting the needs of his village to Kabul. He thanked us for visiting his village and again apologized for the condition of the bridge. His workers had made the repair, and we were able to drive our vehicles back across the bridge with no problems. Simpson was going to have to report the loss of the vehicle to his command, since it belonged to him. I also reported the incident on my SITREP that night. A few days later, I talked with Kellogg. The 412th Civil Affairs was bringing its own vehicles and didn't need the Mercedes, so we decided that we would replace the Hilux with the Mercedes.

The village elder of Zair Som, Abdul Bagui, was a very persistent person. He would come to the firebase every day to talk to us. Sometimes he brought some workers with him, and sometimes he worked at the base. At first I didn't like him. I called him the used car salesman, but after awhile I got to where I did like him. One day he was working at the firebase and walked by our tent as we were watching a movie. It was the first time he had ever seen a television. He was mesmerized by it. I invited him into our tent to watch the movie. It was fun to watch his expression, as he was so excited. Nino was a big fan of "SpongeBob SquarePants"; he had a DVD full of SpongeBob episodes. Nino put in that DVD and played it for Abdul. He sat there, laughed, and laughed at it. When it was over, he thanked us for letting him watch it and invited us to his place for dinner.

He was very appreciative for what we were doing for the people of the valley. He said it was the first time that his wife and daughter had seen a doctor. They were both suffering from malaria but now were doing much better. He said we were much different from the Russians—they killed many people in the valley, but we were there to help the people. After our meal, I asked Abdul to take us to where he wanted the pedestrian bridge built. Steve, Nino, Tim, and I looked the location over. I knew it would be a long time before Kabul could do anything, and I asked them if they thought we could build it ourselves. The engineers had left lot of extra supplies. We could use the Hesco barriers as a base, and we had extra plywood that we could use for the deck. All we needed were logs for the stringers. Abdul knew where we could get long tree logs. We decided that we could build the bridge. We told Abdul we would build him a bridge, but he was going to have to supply us with some workers. Abdul told us the whole village would help us.

The next couple of days, we gathered up the supplies and delivered them to the village. We used three Hesco barriers as the support. one at each end and one in the middle. We had Abdul's work crew fill them with rocks. We then placed the logs on top of the barriers. The engineers left us twenty bags of cement. We used the cement to secure the logs on top of the barriers, then we covered the logs with the plywood. It took us three days to build the bridge. We could have done it in two, but we had to keep stopping to drink tea. About every half hour, someone would bring us tea, so we would stop and drink it with them. When we poured the cement, they were all fascinated with it. They couldn't believe how hard and strong it was. I told them if they used this to build their houses, they would last a lot longer. When we finished the bridge, the whole village came out and celebrated. It was a great feeling to know we did something to help the people of Zair Som. The motto of Civil Affairs is "To Win Hearts and Minds." We truly did that in Zair Som.

18

The Caves

Simpson and his team received orders on April 28, 2003, to return to Bagram on the helicopter that was delivering their replacements, ODA 313 1st Battalion 3rd Special Forces Group. Captain Mark Hunt, twenty-six years old and a recent graduate of Special Forces school, was the commander of ODA 313. This was his first combat mission, and he was eager to get into the fight. His team sergeant was thirty-eight-year-old Master Sergeant John Guzzo. Guzzo was an experienced veteran with twenty years in the Army, fifteen of them as a Green Beret.

This was Guzzo's second combat tour in Afghanistan. He had seen plenty of fighting during his first tour, when his team participated in Operation Anaconda in the Shahi Kot Valley. Anaconda was the first large-scale battle in Afghanistan involving the United States military, since the battle of Tora Bora in December 2001. Guzzo's team battled entrenched Taliban and Al-Qaeda forces on the mountains of the Shahi Kot Valley. Guzzo wasn't very excited to be back in Afghanistan so soon.

The 3rd Group's first tour was February 2002 to September 2002. They were replaced by the 20th Group in September, and now, seven months later, they were back replacing the 20th Group. The rumor was that the 3rd Group did not have a good first tour, and they were being sent back to get it right. Several investigations were conducted by the CID (Criminal Investigation Division) of wrongdoings during their first deployment. When we were in Lwara, two CID agents came out to the base to investigate a shooting of a civilian that happened there, while the 3rd Group was in charge of the firebase. The soldiers who were involved in the shooting were eventually cleared, and no charges were filed.

We were tasked with orienting the new team. Simpson had left an assessment of the Madr and Kahmard valleys for Hunt and his team. We spent the next week taking Hunt and his team around to the villages in the AO and introducing them to the various village elders.

Throughout the Madr and Kahmard Valleys, there were literally hundreds and hundreds of caves. During our tour of the Madr Valley with Hunt and his team, we visited the village of Do Ru and introduced Hunt to Eshan Sahib, the village elder of Do Ru and senior elder of Madr Valley. Sahib was a former leader of the Mujahedeen during the Russian occupation. In the assessment of the Madr and Kahmard Valleys that Simpson left for Hunt there was the need to conduct a search of the cave complexes in the two valleys. During the Med Cap, Simpson had received information that there were several weapon caches hidden in the caves. Simpson was concerned that these weapons could be used by Rahmatullah supporters. He listed this as one of the top priorities that needed to be addressed by the new team.

Hunt asked Sahib what he knew about the caves and the possibility of weapons being hidden in them. Sahib told us that, when he was a Mujahedeen fighting the Russians, they would ambush a Russian patrol then disappear into the caves. They would use the connecting tunnels to move throughout the valley virtually unmolested. They stored their weapons and ammunition in strategic locations throughout the valley. He said there were probably still weapons stored in some of the caves, but he wasn't sure where. We thanked Sahib for his hospitality, and he in turn thanked us for what we were doing for the people of the valley.

Major Khan, Hunt, Guzzo, Steve, and I got together in the OP center to discuss the caves. There was a series of cave complexes near the village of Paghmania that we decided to investigate first. Major Khan wanted to talk with Gul Agha, the village elder of Paghmania, to see what he knew of the caves and if there were any minefields in the area. The locals were all very aware of where the minefields were located. We had several boxes of school supplies and cases of undistributed humanitarian food packets. Steve thought this would be a good opportunity to get rid of those supplies. It always helped to give an elder something for his village when we were looking for information.

We loaded our vehicles with the supplies and made the twenty-minute trip to Paghmania. Elder Agha was very happy to see us. Paghmania was an average-size village with approximately 150 families. There were two small schools, one for boys and one for girls. We had book bags filled with pencils, crayons, paper, coloring books, and erasers for each student. The children were very excited as they dove into the bags to see what was in them. They had never had their own school supplies before. They looked with amazement as they thumbed through the coloring book. There were pictures of sailboats, airplanes, tractors, cars, and animals—things that these children had never seen before. They didn't know how to use the book or the crayons. I explained to the children that we were from America, and the pictures in the book were things that we had in America. I then demonstrated how to use the crayons to color the pictures. They took the crayons out and scribbled on the book. They would then show each other the color it made. The smiles on their faces and their giggles made us as happy as they were. We gave the extra bags to the teachers. I could tell they wanted to use the crayons, too, and if they got new students, they had something to give them.

We brought enough food packets for each family to receive two. We left these with Agha to distribute. Agha was very happy with everything we were doing for his village, and he invited us to eat dinner with him. We went to his house, which was located in the center of the village. It was just like every other house we had been in—dirt floor, no furniture, no lights, and a musty smell. He fed us the Afghan staple of bread, rice, and goat meat.

This was Hunt's first time eating Afghan cuisine. Guzzo was familiar with the whole Afghan process of eating a meal. As always, Aga had one of his sons bring out a pitcher of murky water that was just drawn from the local creek. The water smelled like a plugged-up gas station toilet. He poured it over our hands and then another son gave us the dirty towel to dry our hands. Hunt had a look of disgust and disbelief on his face as he smelled his hands after washing them in the murky water. We laughed at his expression, and I tossed him my bottle of hand sanitizer and told him he might want to start carrying one of these with him. Agha had a special treat for us to start our meal off—freshly made yogurt. Anytime we were offered yogurt, we knew we had made a big hit with an elder. This yogurt was nothing like the cold, sweetened, fruity yogurt we buy in a grocery store. This yogurt is served warm and is very bitter. Agha's son brought out a big bowl with one spoon. Major Khan and Sultan were very excited to see the yogurt, and they each took a big spoonful. Hunt was sitting next to Sultan, and they passed the bowl to him. I knew better than to eat the yogurt. When yogurt is served and passed to me, I just pass it on to the person next to me. Unfortunately for Hunt, he didn't know better, and we figured he needed to learn the way we did—by taking a spoonful of it. We all looked at each other and had a hard time not laughing, because we knew what was going to happen next. He put a big spoonful of yogurt in his mouth and he began to gag. I thought he was going to vomit right there. He put his hand over his mouth in an attempt to muffle his gagging sounds. He managed to finally swallow what was left in his mouth; the rest of it had run down his chin. Guzzo looked over to him and said, "Oh, by the way, don't eat the yogurt."

"You could have told me that a little sooner."

"Welcome to Afghanistan. That was how I learned not to eat the yogurt."

"Consider yourself lucky. Our initiation came in the form of a barrage of 107-mm rockets," I said.

"I don't know what is more dangerous, a rocket attack or this yogurt," replied Hunt.

After our dinner, we asked Agha what he knew about the caves. He said he hadn't been up in the mountains for many years, so he wasn't sure what was in the caves. We asked him if he knew of any minefields in the area. He said there were some in the area, so he would have his son, Safieullah, who was familiar with the minefields, guide us up the mountain away from them. We thanked him for his hospitality and headed back to the firebase where we planned our mission to the caves for the next day.

There was a series of ten caves in the mountains surrounding Paghmania at an elevation of approximately twelve thousand feet. It was a one-mile trek of a relentlessly steep and narrow trail up the mountain that ran along a ridge. The steep cliffs surrounding the trail were dizzying. At points along the trail, the footing became very dangerous with loose rock. We were loaded down with our body armor, weapons, and ammunition, which added an extra fifty pounds. As we stopped periodically to catch our breath, I looked around. The views were spectacular. In every direction that I looked, the mountains dominated the horizon with their snow-clad pyramids.

After nearly an hour's hike up the mountain, we made it to the caves. The first three caves were small and shallow. We could barely stand up in them, and they were no more than fifteen feet deep. We found nothing in these caves. The remaining caves were much larger; some were as deep as sixty feet. In one cave, we found human skeletal remains. Safieullah told us that the Russians executed the families of the Mujahedeen fighters and disposed of the bodies in the caves. In other caves, we found musical instruments, pictures, paintings, and statutes. These were items that were forbidden under Taliban law. Safieullah explained that the locals hid these items from the Taliban in the caves. In one cave, we found a wooden box containing several statutes that appeared to be Egyptian. These turned out to be ancient Egyptian statutes dating back to Alexander the Great. They belonged to the National Museum in Kabul but, soon after the Taliban took control, were smuggled out of Kabul and hidden in the cave for safekeeping. We notified Bagram of our find, and they were going to make arrangements for us to return them to Kabul. We gave the instruments, pictures, and paintings to Gul Agha. Major Khan told him to return them to the owners, as they were no longer forbidden.

We didn't find any weapon caches that day, but what we did find showed us how much suffering the Afghan people had to endure over the past twenty years. When we returned those items to Gul Agha, he hugged us and thanked us. Major Khan told Gul Agha that the dark days of Afghanistan were over, and this was a new beginning; they didn't have to fear the Taliban or warlords anymore. As I listened to Major Khan, I thought to myself that I would like to believe him, but I knew better. The Taliban was far from beaten in the southeast. We had to pull out of Lwara because we didn't have enough troops or resources to continue the fight, and now, with another war in Iraq, it would be a long time before we could fully defeat the Taliban. With their safe haven in Pakistan, they would grow stronger, making it even more difficult to defeat them.

Kellogg sent me a message that Major General Dan McNeill was going to visit the firebase in two days. He was bringing a representative from the National Museum with him to retrieve the antiquities that we found. He was also bringing some reporters who were working on a story on the success of the Afghan National Army in the Madr and Kahmard valleys. Since I was the senior ranking officer, I was the one designated to give him the briefing. He wanted to be briefed on Operation Roll Tide and the subsequent civil military operations that we had carried out in conjunction with the Afghan National Army. He also wanted to meet with local elders to discuss their needs.

While briefing the general, we had to be in full uniform, clean shaven, and sporting a military haircut. Steve, Tim, Nino, and I had full beards; the last time we shaved was in February, and it was now the first of May. I had Major Khan go to the different villages and invite all the elders to meet with General McNeill. I began working on a PowerPoint briefing, and that night we went through the process of shaving our beards.

The elders began arriving at the firebase at 10:00 A.M. General McNeill was scheduled to arrive by noon. Major Khan had his cook prepare a meal for the elders, General McNeill, and his staff. He was to meet with the elders while we ate, then we would move to the Op center for the briefing. After the briefing, the representative would receive the antiquities, and they would be back on the helicopter no later than 2:00 P.M. Typically, if I had to give a briefing to a lieutenant general, I would be extremely nervous. I would rehearse the briefing over and over again, making sure that I followed the correct protocol. This time I wasn't one bit nervous; I never even rehearsed the briefing. I didn't care if I didn't follow the correct protocol; my tour of duty was almost up, and I would be going home soon. Then I was retiring from the Army. I was actually looking forward to meeting the general and showing him what we had accomplished.

The general arrived right on time. He had quite a large entourage with him, which is exactly what I expected. I greeted the general with a salute and welcomed him to Firebase Romero. It was the first time that I had saluted anyone since I arrived in Afghanistan. He returned my salute, and we shook hands. I introduced him to Major Khan, and he took the general on a quick review of his soldiers. General McNeill thanked the soldiers for their service to Afghanistan, and he told them Afghanistan was a better place now because of them. As the general was talking to the ANA, the general's Chief of Staff, Colonel Jerry McBride, pulled me aside to make sure I was ready for the briefing. The general had a very tight itinerary, and he couldn't afford to get behind. I told him we were all set and he would be back on his bird in plenty of time. When the general finished with the ANA, I walked him through the receiving line of the village elders. After he shook hands with all the elders, we sat down, and the ANA served us the meal of rice and goat meat. As we ate, the general talked about President Karzai and his commitment to rebuild Afghanistan. He also explained to them that the Afghan National Army was the legitimate military force of Afghanistan and that they will be permanently stationed in the valley, providing security for their villages. After we finished eating, the general thanked the elders for coming, and he told them he would be back again to check on how things are progressing in the Madr and Kahmard valleys.

We walked over to the Op center, where I briefed the general on Operation Roll Tide and our other Civil Military Operations. I started the briefing with an overview of Operation Roll Tide. I explained to the general that the Afghan National Army was well prepared for the mission, that their soldiers were highly motivated and well disciplined, and that they were responsible for our success with the mission. I then went over all the civil military projects that we worked on. One of the main concerns in the valley was the lack of medical care. I showed him pictures of our Med Cap and gave him the number of people and animals that were treated. My recommendation was that the Army continue the med caps on a regular basis. I then went over the schools we supported, the bridge we built, and the water wells and road projects that we submitted. I also briefed the general on the difficulties that we faced with the loss of support due to the war in Iraq. I told him how we were short on supplies and described the fiasco we had experienced on the air drop. As I was talking about the air drop, I looked over to Colonel McBride, and he was giving me a dirty look. Obviously, he didn't like me telling the general about the problems we had. It would probably make more work for McBride, because the general would tell him to fix it. I didn't care if McBride didn't like it; I had the general's ear, and I was going to tell him the way it was. I didn't have to play the political game now. When the briefing was over, General McNeill thanked me for a great briefing. He particularly liked how candid I was with the problems we faced. He told me he would have his staff look into the way Bagram was supporting their Forward Operating Bases. He acknowledged that the war in Iraq had changed the way we fight the war in Afghanistan, but there was no reason for us to run short on supplies. It was the easiest briefing I had ever done.

After briefing General McNeill, the representative from the National Museum accepted the statutes that we found in the cave from Major Khan. The representative told the reporters that these statutes were national treasures of Afghanistan. They were in the process of rebuilding the museum, and these statutes would be back on display in the very near future. The general and his entourage got back on the helicopter and took off at exactly 2:00 P.M., right on schedule. With the briefing over, now we could focus on our most important mission—going home.

19

Going Home

We could hear the familiar roar of the helicopter rotor blades off in the distance. Our excitement grew as the roar got louder the closer they got. This was nothing new; we had been through many resupplies over the past ten months, but this one had a special meaning—our replacements were on it. This had been a long year, and there were times when I thought I wouldn't make it to see this day. But we survived, and now the helicopter was touching down with a new team to carry on the mission.

The 412th Civil Affairs, from Columbus, Ohio, was replacing us. As the team got off the helicopter, we quickly loaded up their equipment and drove them to the firebase. The four-man team was commanded by Major Tom Stark, a thirty-eight-year-old banker from Columbus, Ohio. His team sergeant was Sergeant First Class Mike Hoobler, a forty-year-old contractor from Columbus. The other two members of the team were Sergeant Rick Smith, twenty-eight-year-old heavy equipment operator, and Specialist Terry McCord, a twenty-year-old college student.

After they got settled in, Steve and I sat down with Stark and Hoobler and went over the orientation process. We soon found out that they were as inexperienced as we had been when we first arrived in Afghanistan; none of them had any previous combat experience. Fortunately for us, we could draw on our law enforcement experience to get us through those tense situations in Lwara. The 412th didn't have that civilian experience to fall back on. They were somewhat overwhelmed with the whole process, as they had arrived in Afghanistan just two days ago. They signed for their equipment, had their briefings, and then were put on a helicopter; and here they were. When we arrived in Bagram, we were fortunate to have Thompson waiting for us. He knew what it was like at the firebase and what equipment we needed for our safety and well-being. He told us that many times throughout his tour that the radios would go down and the only way to communicate with Bagram was with a satellite phone. He told us about an ambush they ran into one day. They tried to radio Bagram for air support, but their radio went down. The only way they could get help was through the satellite phone. Thompson made sure that we got a satellite phone. Unfortunately for the 412th, they didn't have a Thompson helping them. All they had helping them was our B-Team, who had spent the entire tour in the safe confines of Bagram. They had no idea what it was like at the forward operating bases or how important it was to have a satellite phone, so Stark didn't get one. I told Stark that he needed to put in a request to his B-Team to get him a satellite phone. When the shit hits the fan and they need to call in for help, the satellite phone may be the difference between surviving an attack or going home in a body bag. I could see as their chins dropped, and by the concerned looks on their faces, that they had no idea what war was really like. But neither did we when we got here.

I told them that the AO here was very permissive, and the locals seemed to be very friendly, but the number-one thing they must learn is that the only ones they can trust here are themselves. No matter how nice the locals seem, do not become lax and lulled into the belief that they are your friends. The enemy here doesn't wear a uniform. They might be nice to your face and feed you a nice meal while, earlier that day, they planted an IED (Improvised Explosive Devise) in the road or set a rocket up to be fired at the firebase. They sat quietly listening to us telling them about some of our experiences in Lwara. I told them we would start visiting the villages in the AO the next day. We didn't have much time for a handoff, as we were getting picked up in three days. We would only have time to visit the villages in the Madr Valley. Hunt and his team would take them to the Kahmard valley.

That night, I introduced Stark and his team to Major Khan, Sultan, and some of the ANA soldiers. I told them that we would be taking Stark and his team out on a visit of the villages in the Madr Valley and that we would need a security detail. Major Khan told us that he would provide us the detail and that he would also accompany us.

The next morning, we took the 412th to the range to test fire their weapons and rehearse how to react to an ambush. They went through the paces and did the rehearsal as if they were back at Fort Bragg. They still hadn't made the connection that they were in a war. I remembered back to when we arrived in Lwara and went through the drill of what to do during a rocket attack. We went through the paces then but didn't make the connection to the importance until the next night, when we really did get rocketed. After that frightening night, we took everything seriously.

The plan was to visit Do Ru, Do Sakh, and Zair Som first, then Paghmania, Ta Tara, and Madr the next day. The ANA took the lead with a vehicle and five soldiers, followed by our two vehicles, then Major Khan's vehicle, and another ANA vehicle with five more soldiers. I explained to Stark this was a typical convoy procedure. The village of Do Ru was located a quarter mile off the roadway. A series of irrigation ditches crossed between cornfields. The ditches and cornfields were located between the roadway and the village and prohibited us from driving up to the village. When we got to Do Ru, the ANA provided a security detail that stayed with the vehicles, then another security detail followed us into the village. It was slow going as we walked on top of the ditches. When we reached the outskirts of the village, we then had to walk down a long, narrow alley to get to the center of the village. I wanted to introduce Stark to Eshan Sahib, the village elder. A river cut through the center of the village; I was pointing out different points of interest to Stark as we waited for Sahib to join us. Major Khan had sent one of his soldiers to get Sahib. I turned around to speak to Steve, and I couldn't believe what I saw. Hoobler was standing off to the side, looking around, and he didn't have his weapon with him.

I went over to him and said, "Where in the hell is your weapon?"

Hoobler stood there for a few seconds and didn't say anything.

He swallowed hard, and his lips quivered as he said, "I forgot it, it's in the vehicle."

"Did you forget where the hell you are? How could you forget your weapon? What are you going to do if we come under attack?" I was so mad, now I knew how Brady felt when Warren walked off in Gayan.

Now Hoobler was shaking as he said, "I'm sorry, I wasn't paying attention."

"Sorry doesn't cut it. Not paying attention will get you killed here. You're not back at your reserve center playing Army; the bullets are real, and there are people here who want nothing more than to kill an American."

Everyone knew I was mad. I didn't make it a habit of yelling at people, but I had to get my point across if these guys were going to survive. Hoobler didn't have much to say the rest of the day as we visited the other villages. Steve said he would watch him like a hawk from now on. That night, when we got back to the firebase, I had a talk with Stark. I made it clear to him that he couldn't afford to have his team members walk off without their weapons. He needed to keep a close eye on Hoobler, and if he continued to make mistakes, put him on the next flight back to Bagram. They could find him a job back in Bagram where he didn't have to worry about carrying his weapon.

The helicopter was scheduled to pick us up at 1:00 P.M. and fly us back to Bagram. We turned all of our equipment over to Stark; the only things we were bringing back to Bagram were our weapons and personal gear. I was able to sign over the satellite phone to Stark along with our computers, cameras, and ammo. We also gave them our TV, VCR, and all the other stuff sent to us to make our lives a little easier. The other thing we were instructed to turn over to them was our blood chit. A blood chit is a silk-like paper that features a dozen different languages and carries a message directed at civilians that says, "I am a citizen of the United States of America. I do not speak your language. Misfortune forces me to seek your assistance in obtaining food, shelter, and protection. Please take me to someone who will provide for my safety and see that I am returned to my people. My government will reward you." I carried it the whole time I was in Afghanistan. Thompson gave me his blood chit when he left, and I was now passing it on to Stark. When I gave Stark the blood chit, I said the same thing to him that Thompson said when he gave it to me.

"I hope you don't have to use this here, because if you do, you're going to be in big trouble. Very few people can read." He looked at it and laughed. We shook hands, and I wished him good luck.

The helicopter circled around Bagram as it prepared to land. As I looked out the window, I couldn't help but notice how much Bagram had grown since we first arrived in September. I could see that there were new buildings going up all over the base. We touched down, and the crew chief dropped the back ramp. Our B-Team was waiting for us; we loaded up the trucks and headed over to the compound. We were the last team from our unit to return to Bagram. It was great seeing everyone again; it had been over nine months since we were all together. We were scheduled to fly out in two days. We had to have everything we were taking back laid out for inspection by the MPs (Military Police) the next morning before we could secure in the Conex storage container. They had to inspect everything to make sure we weren't taking any unauthorized equipment home. Several soldiers were caught trying to smuggle an AK-47 home. They were charged with unlawful possession of firearms and received a dishonorable discharge from the Army.

The next day, the MPs came through and inspected us then observed us as we packed the Conex. After they were packed, the MPs put a seal on the door, clearing it for shipping. The rest of the day, we sat around, swapped stories, and played cards. Our flight was scheduled to take off at 1:30 A.M.

As we were preparing for takeoff, the pilot came on and told us that we would be following the same procedures for takeoff as we did for landing at Bagram. As the C-17 taxied down the runway, the lights went off, and the plane accelerated and lifted off. The pilot put the plane in a very steep takeoff. Our ears were popping. The plane rolled hard to the right then hard to the left, and it was like being on a roller coaster. Finally, the plane leveled out, the lights came on, and the pilot came on and said we had just left Afghanistan airspace. Everyone in the plane let out a big cheer. He told us that we would be stopping in Germany to refuel then off to Pope Air Force Base, North Carolina. It was going to be about a twenty-hour flight, but we didn't care, because we were on our way home.

At 1:23 P.M. on May 21, 2003, the C-17 touched down at Pope Air Force Base. Pope Airbase was connected to Fort Bragg; it was the airbase that the 82nd Airborne used. I didn't know what to expect when we got off the airplane. I remembered watching troops returning home from Desert Storm and seeing large crowds and welcome-home banners waiting for them. I also remember watching the same thing for the troops returning home from Grenada and Panama. I wondered if the same thing was awaiting us.

The ramp in the back of the plane dropped down, and we walked off. What a great feeling knowing that I didn't have to go back! I looked around the tarmac for our welcome, but no one was here waiting for us or welcoming us home. We picked up our gear and walked over to the staging area. The staging area is where the airborne soldiers wait to board the aircraft. I couldn't believe it—there wasn't even anybody here to pick us up. Kellogg walked over to a pay phone to try to call somebody from Bragg to pick us up. Most of us had just returned from the firebases only two days before. Our uniforms were worn and tattered after nine months in combat. We had put our baseball caps away and were wearing our Army-issued Desert Boonie hats. It had been over two hours, and still no one had picked us up.

A colonel from another Army unit came walking through the staging area while we were waiting. His uniform was nicely pressed, and his boots were highly polished. He looked at us with a disgusting look on his face. He was wearing Quartermaster Branch Insignia, which meant he had some cushy job in the rear. I could tell he had never been in a combat zone, because he wasn't wearing a combat patch. When soldiers are deployed in a designated combat zone, they are then authorized to wear the unit patch of the unit they were in combat with, on their right shoulder. We were attached to the 20th Special Forces Group, so we wore the Special Forces unit patch on our right shoulder. Of all the badges that a soldier can earn in the Army, a combat patch is the most coveted.

The colonel asked who our commanding officer was. Kellogg spoke up and said he was. He told Kellogg that his soldiers looked like a ragtag, undisciplined, gaggle, and if they were his soldiers, he would be ashamed of their appearance. He went on to say that our hats were only authorized to be worn while we were in the field. We weren't in the proper uniform, because we didn't have name tapes, rank, or unit patches sewn on them. He wanted to know what unit we were with, because he was going to report us to our chain of command. Kellogg said, "Thank you for bringing that to my attention sir, we are the 403rd Civil Affairs. We just got off the plane from a nine-month combat deployment in Afghanistan with the Special Forces. My soldiers have been living in conditions that you are not familiar with, but if we ever get picked up and taken to our barracks we will make the necessary corrections." After being put in his place, the colonel walked off. I thought to myself, "What a great welcoming home that was."

After a two-and-a-half-hour wait, we were finally picked up and trucked over to the old post and assigned to one of the old World War II barracks. These barracks were over sixty years old. They were originally built as temporary housing, but the Army was still using them. I wasn't very happy being back in these old barracks, but I didn't think we would be here much more than a week. We had running water, toilets, showers, and beds; it was more than we had for the last nine months. We got settled in and met with Kellogg that night. It was the Thursday before Memorial Day weekend. We couldn't begin turning in our equipment until Tuesday, so Kellogg gave us the weekend off; we didn't have to report back until Tuesday morning at 8:00 A.M. He told us he would have a schedule for us then. We had to turn in all the field gear that we signed for at Fort Bragg. Then we had to clear the operations fund, listen to a briefing from the Veterans Administration, and get an out-processing physical. If everything went smoothly, we should be done by the end of the following week.

The next morning, I rented a car and drove home for the Memorial Day weekend. It was a twelve-hour drive, and I didn't get home until 10:00 P.M. I walked in the backdoor, and Lorrie ran up and gave me a big hug. It was so good to be back home, and this time I was home to stay. Just before I left for Afghanistan, we purchased a fully trained guard dog. We only had him a few weeks before I left, then I spent ten days with him when I was home on leave six months ago. I don't think he was as happy to see me as Lorrie was. He had bonded with her, and now that I was here, I think he was quite annoyed with me being home. Every time I would get close to Lorrie, he would try to get between us. If Lorrie and I walked upstairs, he would push by me and walk up the stairs ahead of me. Over time, he got better with me, but he never bonded with me as he did with her.

We went upstairs and woke the kids; they jumped into my arms and grabbed me around the neck. The kids took me around the house and showed me all the rugs and souvenirs that I had sent home over the past nine months. Lorrie then walked me around the house too, and showed me all the work she had done on the house. Her plan was to have it done before I came home so I could just enjoy spending time with her and the boys. We spent the rest of the weekend visiting families and friends.

The Army was going to release us from stop loss ninety days after we were released from active duty. This meant that, in October 2003, I would be able to retire from the Army. There was no question that I was going to retire. I thought I had it rough spending nine months in combat, but what Lorrie had to go through—raising three boys and taking care of our house with little support from the Army and not knowing what was happening to me—was just as hard as what I went through. We had a family support group back at the unit, which was great for the families who lived in the Syracuse area, but we lived 140 miles away from the unit, and the family support group wasn't able to help her. During most of my deployment, I was the only service member in the area deployed. A lot of people didn't even know a war was still going on. While I was gone, our oldest son, Seth, had a lot of problems in school. He was ten years old at the time and was well aware of what I was doing. He was having difficulty paying attention in class. When his teacher questioned him why he wasn't paying attention, he tried to explain to her about his daddy fighting in the war. She abruptly told him that the war was over a long time ago, and he had better get his act together. Seth started becoming physically ill over having to go to school. Lorrie had to go to the school to try to educate them that there indeed was still a war going on and how our children were affected by it.

While dealing with the school, our new house brought problems that we weren't prepared for. The winter of 2002 to 2003 was a very cold winter. One cold, January night, Lorrie woke up to find the house stone cold—the furnace had quit. She had to search through the phone book at 2:00 A.M. to find someone who would make an emergency house call in the middle of the night. She had the kids bundled up, then a strange repairman came to the door. He took one look at the dog jumping at the door, ran back to his truck, and started to leave. Lorrie had to run down the driveway to catch him before he left. She had to maintain our cars, mow the lawn in summer, shovel the driveway in winter, pay the bills, and be both a mom and dad to the kids. Our dream home had become a burden for a single mom.

It wasn't until April 2003, one month before I came home, that the Red Cross started a support group locally for wives of deployed service members. There was a Marine Reserve Unit in Syracuse that deployed to Iraq in February, and it had several members living in our area. Although it was late getting started, Lorrie and the kids were grateful to finally have support and not feel alone.

As I was getting ready to head back to Fort Bragg, I told Lorrie if everything goes as planned, I should be home within a week. I really didn't want to leave, but I just wanted to get everything turned in and come home for good. I reported back to Fort Bragg on Tuesday morning and found out that we had a packed schedule. Over the next four days, everything went really smooth. I cleared my operation fund with no problems, we got all of our equipment turned in without a hitch, and we finished up the week with our briefings and physicals. Now all we had to get was our orders releasing us from active duty. It was late Friday afternoon when we finished with our physicals, so we knew we wouldn't get the orders until Monday; it seemed that everything shut down on the weekends. I didn't like the idea of spending the weekend at Fort Bragg. It was getting hot, and our barracks weren't air conditioned. The barracks were in terrible condition. Only half the showers and toilets worked. I didn't like it, but I decided that a couple more days wouldn't hurt me. I called home and told Lorrie that I wasn't coming home yet. We had to wait to get our orders releasing us from active duty, and we weren't going to get them until Monday. She wasn't very happy, as she and the kids really wanted me home, but there wasn't anything we could do about it other than wait. Kellogg gave us the weekend off, but we didn't have much to do. We went to the mall in Fayetteville and watched a movie every day. It was air conditioned, and it helped kill time. We were all looking forward to Monday and getting our orders releasing us from active duty.

At our formation Monday morning, Kellogg said he didn't have any word yet, but he was heading over to the headquarters building and maybe would have some word for us after lunch. He released us until our next formation at 1:00 P.M. I wasn't expecting any word that early in the morning, as I figured he would get the orders later in the morning and give us the plan for leaving at the afternoon formation. As soon as we got the orders, we could make our flight reservations. I was hoping to fly out the next day. At the 1:00 P.M. formation, Kellogg said the orders hadn't been cut yet. Maybe at our evening formation he would have some information. I was really disgusted, as we were finished turning in all of our equipment, and everything on our demobilization check list was completed. We were just waiting for some private to write the orders and some colonel to sign them. At the evening formation, the news was the same, no orders.

The next four days brought the same news: no orders. We had now spent a week with nothing to do. There was absolutely no reason for it. Every night, I would call home. Lorrie would ask me when I was coming home, and I had to tell her I didn't know. We couldn't understand why we weren't being released. One night, as I was talking to Lorrie on the phone, she was out in our back yard watching the kids playing on the swing set. She stepped into a hole one of the kids had dug to catch bad guys who might be walking in the yard and severely sprained her ankle. That Friday night, after our formation at 5:00 P.M., I made the twelve-hour drive home to help her around the house. I waited until Sunday night, after the kids went to bed, to drive back to Fort Bragg. I was hoping for some good news at the Monday formation, but as usual, there wasn't any.

The days of waiting for our release from active duty turned into weeks. I couldn't understand why the Army was treating us like this.

We had a tremendously successful tour of duty. It was now four weeks since our arrival back to the United States, and there was still no word on our release. Our families were furious with the Army. Several of them called Special Operations Headquarters in Fort Bragg, but they were given no information on our release. Our families then began calling their congressman and asking them for help. Lorrie called our congressman, Amory Houghton, and his staff member told her they would look into it. The Army got several inquiries from the congressmen on our status. There was talk of a formal Congressional Inquiry on our situation.

During the four weeks since our return to the United States, no one from our higher headquarters ever paid us a visit to welcome us home or thanked us for our tour of duty. Then one Tuesday morning, as we were beginning our fifth week at Fort Bragg, we got the word that our brigade commander, Colonel Mitch McManus of the 354th Civil Affairs Brigade, was going to meet with us at the afternoon formation. Finally, we were going to get some information. We figured he knew when we were going to be released and would be telling us that at the formation. That afternoon, at 1:00 P.M., we had our formation in front of the barracks. I didn't know anything about McManus, since he had taken over command of the brigade while we were in Afghanistan. As he walked up in front of the formation, I was eagerly awaiting to hear the news. I was sure we would have to listen to him first welcome us home and congratulate us on a fine tour, then tell us when we were being released. I thought it would have been nice for him to visit us and welcome us back during the first day or two instead of waiting this long. If I were the brigade commander, I would have been waiting for my troops as they got off the airplane to welcome them back.

As the colonel began to speak, there was no welcome back, no congratulations on a fine tour, and no "thank you" for your service to our country. He started out with, "I am going to tell you people something right now, you need to tell your families to stop calling their congressmen and having them involved in your release. If this goes to a congressional inquiry, you will be stuck here at least six months as they drag the inquiry out." One of our soldiers raised his hand. "What, soldier?" the colonel asked.

"Why are we not being released? It would help if our families had some information."

"If the Army wanted you to know why you're not being released, they would tell you. I'm going to tell you again: tell your families to stop calling their congressmen, and I am giving all of you an order—you are not allowed to call your congressman."

With that the colonel walked off. So much for the welcome home. Obviously, they were getting a lot of heat from the congressmen. The colonel couldn't give us an order to not to talk to our congressman. As soon as he left, everyone pulled out their cell phones and called home. I called Lorrie and told her, and she immediately called Congressman Houghton's office and related what we were just told. I had been around the Army too long. I knew the colonel was trying to blow smoke up our asses. There was no way the Army would keep us here if there were a congressional inquiry. What our families were doing was working, and they kept up the pressure.

The next day, our orders amazingly came through, and we were being released the next day. Finally, our tour was over. We were flying home on Thursday, then we had two days of duty at the reserve center. We had more equipment to turn in there, and we were going to have an awards ceremony. It wasn't until a few months later that I found out why we weren't released right away. During our deployment, we were required to take malaria medicine every week. The medicine that we took was Mefloquine, sometimes referred to by its trade name of Lariam. The problem with Mefloquine was that it had severe adverse and sometimes permanent side effects. It was known to cause severe depression, anxiety, paranoia, nightmares, insomnia, and suicidal ideation. Soon after soldiers returned from Afghanistan, in the summer of 2002, there was a rash of domestic killings by soldiers at Fort Bragg. The Army soon decided that they didn't want to release soldiers until the Mefloquine was out of their systems and they were sure we weren't suffering any side effects. It took a month for it to get out of our system. We were never told about the side effects of Mefloquine before we started taking it, nor were we ever told about it when we returned. The Army tried to keep it a secret from us, which was why we were never told why we weren't being released. The Army has since quit giving Mefloquine as the antimalarial drug and has switched to Doxycycline.

That Thursday, we flew home for good. Lorrie and the kids met me at the airport along with a local television station that was doing a story on my return home from Afghanistan. I think they were expecting to see Lorrie and the kids running and jumping into my arms because they hadn't seen me in a year. What the television news crew didn't know was that I had been coming home every weekend for the past month, so when I walked off the airplane, it was pretty uneventful—just, "Hi, how was your flight, lets get our luggage and get out of here." The next day, we reported to the reserve center and spent the day turning in the remainder of our equipment. I filled out my request for retirement, effective that October. It was a strange time at the reserve center. In previous deployments to the Persian Gulf and Bosnia, when the soldiers returned home there, was a big celebration. This time there was no celebration. There were still members of the unit in Afghanistan, and the remainder of the unit that didn't go to Afghanistan was sent to Iraq.

The next day was our last official day of duty for Operation Enduring Freedom, and we finished it with an awards ceremony. It had been a long 393 days of active duty. Our small team of twenty-five soldiers performed a mission that we were never trained for under the most extreme and harsh conditions. We deployed to the most dangerous place in the world to defend freedom and help rebuild a country that had suffered through decades of war. When our soldiers came in contact with the enemy, they responded with courage and valor. Our unit successfully completed every task and mission assigned to us, and in doing so we earned the respect and admiration of the Special Forces teams that we supported.

Our success didn't go unnoticed by the Department of Defense. Our unit was awarded the Joint Meritorious Unit Award. It is the second highest unit decoration that can be bestowed upon a military unit, and it is the only unit citation awarded by the Department of Defense. All soldiers were awarded the Global War on Terrorism Expeditionary Medal for deployment to Afghanistan and the Armed Forces Reserve Medal with Mobilization device for being a member of the Army Reserve unit called to active duty. There were also several individual medals awarded. Six soldiers were awarded the Joint Services Achievement Medal for distinguishing themselves by outstanding performance of duty and meritorious achievement. Five soldiers were awarded the Army Commendation Medals for their heroic actions in direct contact with an enemy force. Four soldiers were awarded the Joint Service Commendation Medal, by the Department of Defense, for their distinguished meritorious service during a joint operation. One soldier was awarded the Purple Heart for the wounds he received during combat operations against an enemy force. Five soldiers were awarded the Bronze Star Medal for their acts of valor, heroism, and extreme meritorious service against an enemy force. The Bronze Star Medal is the United States military's fourth highest award for valor. Fifteen soldiers were awarded the Combat Action Badge for actively engaging an enemy force. Tim and Nino received the Army Commendation Medal, while Steve and I were awarded the Bronze Star Medal. We were all awarded the Combat Action Badge.

The awards and decorations represented the dedication, hard work, and sacrifices that the soldiers of the 403rd Civil Affairs made in defense of freedom. The war in Afghanistan is now into its eighth year, with soldiers making multiple deployments to Afghanistan. The Taliban has grown strong over the past seven years as the United States made the war in Iraq its top priority. Now, as the forces begin their withdrawal from Iraq, the priority has shifted back to Afghanistan. The United States will now have to deal with an enemy that has learned how to fight us. This will not be an easy war to win, but with soldiers like those of the 403rd, the United States will prevail.

Breinigsville, PA USA
11 July 2010

241558BV00002B/6/P

9 781608 609185